ALSO BY CHRIS CRUTCHER

Whale Talk

Ironman

Staying Fat for Sarah Byrnes

Athletic Shorts

Chinese Handcuffs

The Crazy Horse Electric Game

Stotan!

Running Loose

KING OF THE MILD FRONTIER

AN ILL-ADVISED AUTOBIOGRAPHY

CHRIS CRUTCHER

A Greenwillow Book

HARPERTEMPEST

An Imprint of HarperCollinsPublishers

Memory is selective and by nature faulty. That statement is probably doubly true for my memory. Add to that my penchant for exaggeration and the fact that I have changed some of the names for obvious reasons, and you have a memoir that may not stand up to close historical scrutiny. So be it.

—C.C.

King of the Mild Frontier:
An Ill-Advised
Autobiography
Copyright © 2003 by
Chris Crutcher
All photographs courtesy
of the author.
All rights reserved. No part
of this book may be used or
reproduced in any manner
whatsoever without written
permission except in the
case of brief quotations embodied in critical articles and reviews.
Printed in the United States of America. For information address
HarperCollins Children's Books, a division of HarperCollins Publishers,
1350 Avenue of the Americas, New York, NY 10019.

Library of Congress Cataloging-in-Publication Data
Crutcher, Chris.
King of the mild frontier : an ill-advised autobiography / by Chris Crutcher.
p. cm.
"Greenwillow Books"
Summary: Chris Crutcher, author of young adult novels such as "Ironman" and
"Whale Talk," as well as short stories, tells of growing up in Cascade, Idaho, and
becoming a writer.
ISBN 0-06-050249-5 (trade) — ISBN 0-06-050250-9 (lib. bdg.)
ISBN 0-06-050251-7 (pbk.)
1. Crutcher, Chris—Juvenile literature. 2. Authors, American—20th century—
Biography—Juvenile literature. 3. Young adult fiction—Authorship—Juvenile
literature. 4. Idaho—Social life and customs—Juvenile literature. [1. Crutcher,
Chris. 2. Authors, American.] I. Title.
PS3553.R786 Z5 2003   2002011224
813'.54—dc21   CIP
                                                                         AC

Typography by Chad W. Beckerman
❖
First HarperTempest edition, 2004
Visit us on the World Wide Web!
www.harpertempest .com

To my brother for going first,
to my sister for bringing up the rear, and to
Paula Whitson for enduring my advances
with uncommon grace. And to the Hirais and
Bilbaos and Nakatanis for giving us their best,
when they didn't always receive the best

Contents

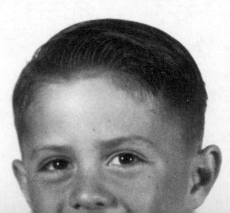

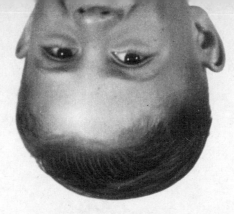

KING OF THE MILD FRONTIER

Fireworks

---◆◇◆---

1

I GREW UP RIDING A ROCKET. If legendary rocket man Wernher von Braun could have harnessed the power of my meteoric temper, we'd have beaten the Russians into space by a good six months. The bits of evidence lay in the wake of my explosive impulsivity like trailer-house pieces behind Hurricane Andrew: broken toys, holes in walls, a crack from top to bottom in a full-length mirror on the bathroom door of "the little house" where I lived until just after my seventh birthday. My dad purposely didn't replace that mirror as a reminder, a monument to me. Subsequently, when he'd see me heating up, he'd point to it and ask one of those questions to which adults never really want an answer: "Are you proud of that?"

"No," I lied, my bottom lip stuck out so far he could have pulled it over my forehead. Of course I was proud of it; I'd had to slam it three times to get it to break.

There was a famous family story about how my temper had been "cured" right around the age of two. It was told by my mother at bridge club, Christmas get-togethers, and you-think-*your*-kids-are-a-pain-in-the-butt afternoon coffee sessions at the Chief Café. It went something like this: "Chris was very difficult to deal with, even at an early age. When things didn't go his way, he would throw himself into the air, kick his legs out from under him, and land hard on the floor. I was afraid he'd hurt himself, so I called Dr. Patterson for advice. Dr. Patterson said, 'Just roll one of those wooden alphabet blocks under him when he goes up. That should take care of it.' So the next time he launched himself, I rolled the block under him, and sure enough he never did it again."

I knew how to keep this story going; I'd done it for years. "But . . . ," I'd say, pointing toward the sky.

"But," my mother went on, "then he began storming into the bathroom and hitting his head against the bathtub when he got mad."

2

"So you called the ever-compassionate Dr. Patterson. . . ." I said.

"And he told me to 'help' him. Just push his head a little harder than he intended."

"And lo and behold . . ."

"He stopped hitting his head against the bathtub."

I'd heard that story all my life, and had been convinced it was a good one, probably because it was about me. On the thousandth telling, however, I sat in a circle in my parents' living room with a group of their friends on Christmas Eve. I was in my mid-thirties, and a thought that should have crossed my mind eons ago pried its way into my consciousness. I said, "Jewell"—the Crutcher kids always called our parents by their first names, which probably deserves closer scrutiny somewhere in this confessional—"do you remember the long crack in the full-length mirror in the bathroom at the little house?"

She frowned. "Of course. Your father wouldn't get it fixed. He left it as a reminder to you."

"Of my temper," I said. "I did that when I was five. Do you remember the hole I kicked in the plasterboard in my bedroom when Paula Whitson asked Frankie Bilbao instead of me to the Sadie Hawkins dance?"

Jewell released a long sigh. "Your father didn't have that fixed, either."

"As a reminder of my temper," I said. "I did that when I was a junior in high school. Do you remember the Volkswagen Bug I had up until about six months ago? With the top that looked as if it had been stung by bees from my punching it from the inside when the electrical system died on a busy street?"

"Yes, dear."

"Crutch wouldn't have had that fixed, either," I said, smiling at my dad. "I did that when I was thirty-three, a little over a year ago. Your story isn't about curing a kid's temper. It's about pissing him off for the rest of his life by rolling blocks under him and whacking his head against the bathtub instead of letting him have his two-year-old rage. Stop telling it."

What my mother didn't say then—and something she and I often talked about years later in the long-term care wing of Valley County Hospital where she had gone to die slowly of emphysema resulting from forty years of a two-and-a-half-pack-a-day habit—was that her fear for me in those days wasn't really that I'd hurt myself bouncing off the floor or banging my head, but that I would grow up with the same temper that stalked and embarrassed and humbled her throughout her own life. Though I couldn't have known it in those early years, it was one of my first experiences with a phenomenon I discovered years later as a child abuse and neglect therapist at the Spokane (Washington) Mental Health Center: Shit rolls downhill.

I'm sure I could audit my early life and find times when my temper was my friend, when it got me through situations where my fear stopped me cold. It certainly helped me survive my early years on the Cascade High School football team where I started out as a 123-pound offensive lineman, when in practice I'd get so angry at the grass stains on my back and the cleat marks on my chest that I'd finally hit someone hard enough to satisfy the coach sufficiently to let me out of the drill. And it got me through my one and only full-tilt fight in junior high school when my embarrassment turned to rage the moment I saw the aforementioned Paula Whitson witness Mike Alkyre cracking my jaw. It took three guys to pull me off, and though I was still the odds-on kid most likely to have my butt kicked by someone from a lower grade, some of them would think twice after watching me cross over into the land of I Don't Care. But far more often than not, my temper brought out behavior that made me embarrassed to show my face around our lumber town of fewer than a thousand citizens for a couple of weeks.

Case in point. The biggest, best holiday (with the possible

exception of Christmas) in Cascade, Idaho, during my childhood years had to be the Fourth of July. A parade led by the town's most prominent horsemen, followed by floats sponsored by virtually every town business, followed by preschoolers on crepe-paper-laden tricycles dodging piles of horseshit that rose to their knees, brought out nearly every ambulatory citizen. The Junior Chamber of Commerce sold hamburgers and pronto pups and cotton candy and ice cream and minor fireworks from plywood stands built on every other street corner. We'd watch or participate in the parade, eat ourselves sick through the lunch hour, then gather at the high-school track, a potholed, quarter-mile dirt road circling the football field, and surrounded by a larger, five-eighths-mile horse-racing track even more pot-holed, where we would participate in foot and bicycle races before settling into the stands to watch the kids and adults from farms and ranches around town, and up from the flat-lands outside Boise and Caldwell, race their horses.

I should back up here and say that pretty girls were my downfall from way before I had hormones enough to govern my embarrassing behavior, and the pretty girl in question here was Carol MacGregor. The MacGregors owned a huge cattle ranch south of town and a medium-sized logging company. Compared to Bill Gates, they would have been Crutchers, but compared to Crutchers, they were Bill Gates. The MacGregor kids got their education in the larger, more cosmopolitan schools of Boise and came north for a couple of weeks each summer to work on the family ranch, ride horses, and dazzle the *Deliverance* kids with their sophistication. We were duly dazzled. Carol's younger brother, Jock, was handsome and cool and funny, and Carol herself was simply otherworldly: pretty and smart, with a flashy smile, in the state of Idaho's tightest jeans, and she rode her horse like it was growing out of her tailbone. At the Fourth of July races she won the barrel race and the stake race and the potato race and the stampede, and brought the towns-folk to their feet in wild applause doing it. The four words that could send the entire preadolescent and adolescent male population of Cascade running for their Brylcreem and combs were "Carol MacGregor's in town."

Well, Carol MacGregor was probably a good five years older than I was and would likely have mistaken me for the sissy little brother of the Pillsbury Doughboy, had Mr. Doughboy been invented yet, but youth is irrepressible and I was convinced that if she saw that my prowess on a bicycle equaled hers on a horse, the rest of the guys in town could pretty much head for the barn alone. So I entered the ten-and-under quarter-mile race on my brand-new purple-

and-white, three-bar Schwinn one-speed, determined to burst onto the Cascade, Idaho, Fourth of July bike-racing scene like Lance Armstrong, who also wasn't invented yet.

It had rained for a full week leading up to that Fourth, and continued to rain, hard enough to send most of the faithful home to begin constructing an ark and turn the dirt track into muddy ooze. A dozen of us took off at the sound of the starter's pistol, and by the time the leader was a hundred yards into the race, he had a fifty-yard lead on me, and my clothes and face were pocked with mud acne. Three-quarters of the way to the finish the *next-to-last guy* had a fifty-yard lead on me, so like an experienced stock-car racer, I cut to the inside to make up ground, inside the little orange flags marking the spots where the track had turned to grainy pudding. As that same second-to-last kid crossed the finish line, I slowed to a crawl at the far turn, standing on the pedals to maintain any forward motion at all. I glanced up to see the other participants pointing back and laughing, at the same time Bob Gardner's voice boomed from the loudspeaker system mounted in the back of my father's pickup near the starting line. "Chris. Get off the bike and push it in. You biked a good race."

In your dreams, Bob Gardner. I'll finish this race *on* the bike or die trying. I may have been dead last, but Carol

MacGregor *had* to be impressed with this degree of what my mother called stick-to-itiveness.

"Chris Crutcher. Get off the bike. Push it on in. You're going slow enough to lose the *next* race."

Ha ha. Pretty funny, Bob Gardner. Now all my weight is on the front pedal as I hear a giant sucking sound reminiscent of a bad guy going down in the quicksand of a Tarzan movie, the bike at a standstill, supported by mud up to midwheel.

"Chris Crutcher, raise your hand if you can hear me."

I'm standing on the pedals now, pulling back on the handlebars with all my might. The townspeople in the bleachers are yelling and clapping, calling me in.

"Chris Crutcher, raise your hand if—"

We have ignition. I did raise my hand, middle finger jutting into the air, as I screamed, "Leave me alone, you big fat shitburger!"

I'm pretty sure I've silenced the people of Cascade on subsequent occasions, but never as creatively nor as completely. The rhythmic beat of raindrops splashing into puddles and the crackling of the loudspeaker system filled the vacuum of sound for a monstrous moment that hung in the air like some breathless angel of death, and my dad fired out of the bleachers like he was nuclear powered, crossed the field in near world-record time, scooped me up under one arm and the bike under the other, and no part of my body touched the good earth until a split second after he slammed on his car brakes in front of the house and pointed toward my upstairs room.

I was allowed out of that room many hours later that night, when I was able to hand him a piece of notebook paper with all the words I could find in "big fat shitburger." Leave it to my dad to turn any incident into an educational opportunity.

In later years I was able to make a few bucks off that temper, as a writer and as a therapist. I gave it to Dillon Hemingway in *Chinese Handcuffs*, Bo Brewster in *Ironman*, and The Tao Jones in *Whale Talk*, and I know I used it more times than I can count to make a psychological connection with any number of my angry students and, later on, clients. In my early days as a therapist, I often made connections with the more rugged of my adult male clients by looking for similarities between their lives and mine, and the thing I landed on most frequently was that temper. I had shamed myself with it enough times in my life to have considerable empathy for those who had done so at the expense of their mates or kids, which made me a natural to work with the "bad guys."

It was clear that most of the time the temper was a product

of self-contempt, aimed outward. The self-contempt came from fear, most often fear of incompetence (which is why my mother should have let me storm around in search of competence when I was still too small to do much damage)—a very difficult condition for a lot of men to admit to. Because the state of fear is such a difficult thing to identify and embrace, it usually gets expressed in anger. The bigger the fear, the greater the self-contempt, therefore the bigger the anger.

I was working in a men's group with a man named Ray, who could have been the poster boy for the paragraph above. He was about six feet, five inches tall and weighed more than 300 pounds, almost always dressed in a cowboy outfit. It was not a Roy Rogers outfit, with which I may have been better equipped to identify from my youth, but a real cowboy outfit: boots and leather pants and a huge belt buckle with long cow horns above the caption YOU CAN HAVE MY COLT FORTY-FIVE WHEN YOU PRY IT FROM MY COLD DEAD FINGERS. Over that he wore a leather long-riders' coat under a broad-brimmed leather hat. Each time he stood in the door surveying the group room, deciding where to sit, I half expected him to throw back the front of the coat, draw his six-guns, and blast the rest of us all over the Painted Desert.

Along with being abusive to his girlfriend and his kids, he had also been a drug dealer. He came to us through Child

Protective Services after leaving her six- and eight-year-old boys locked alone in a trailer house early one morning while he went out and took care of some business. The kids' mother was in the hospital delivering *his* firstborn. He had loosened up enough in the group to talk freely and had been bragging about replacing all physical punishment of the kids with "time out."

I said, "Tell me how 'time out' works at your place."

"Well, I modified it a little. You guys don't seem to know how important it is for a kid to know why he's *in* there."

I said it again. "Tell me how 'time out' works."

"I put 'em in the corner," he said, "nose pressed in the crack, and stand just behind 'em and tell 'em, in a real calm voice, why they're there. When they can repeat it back word for word, and apologize, I let 'em out. Haven't hit a one of 'em since I started doin' that."

I said, "So it's effective?"

"Damned effective, counselor. They get a little pissed at first, sometimes they bawl, especially the older one—he ain't as tough as his brother—but finally they come around."

"How long does it usually take for them to come around?"

"It can be a little rugged. Longest so far is a couple hours. Kids got to learn respect, however long it takes."

A temper creating a temper. I said, "Let's play a little

game. It's just role playing, not anything serious."

"What's the game?" he said cautiously.

"Go over and stand in the corner, with your nose in the crack," I said.

"Get real."

"It's just a game," I said. "Go ahead. Indulge me."

"Kiss my ass."

The other guys in the group started to fidget.

"Okay," I said, "we'll do it a different way. Two Wednesdays from now I'm going into court to testify as to your progress in therapy. What we're doing right now is therapy. I'm asking you to go stand in the corner. You don't do what I say, I tell the truth in court."

"You son of a—"

I put up a finger. "Uh-uh," I said. "That won't help you out. Now go stand in the corner."

Ray got up . . . and up and up. I didn't have to close my eyes to imagine what it must have been like for either of his girlfriend's boys to be stuck in the corner with Ray behind him. This guy blocked out the sun.

This may be as close to the very edge as I ever got doing therapy. He believed I had the power over the kids' return home, and though he didn't like them all that much, if he failed in therapy it meant he'd have to move out for the kids to be returned, which also meant he couldn't live with his *own* newborn, who he had promised us was going to be way tougher than either of these two boys. High stakes.

So Ray stood in the corner and I moved in behind him, though I'm sure I gave him a lot more room than he gave either of the boys because I did not want to be a headline in tomorrow morning's *Spokesman Review*. "Now maybe you'd like to think about what got you here."

He stood quiet.

"I've been running this group for seven years," I said. "I guess I know what I'm doing. I'd like a little more respect. Maybe you can tell me what got you in this corner." (If you haven't seen me, you need to know I'm *way* too skinny to be doing this.)

Ray's fists opened and closed, either of them bigger than my head.

"Listen, man, you can get out of this corner anytime you want. All you have to do is tell me what got you here. And I think an apology to the group might be in order. We've wasted a lot of time." My back was to the rest of the group, but it was so quiet I could almost hear their heads shaking: *No, no. No apology needed here.*

Sweat broke out on the back of Ray's neck and he started to twitch, and even I knew one more step was beyond his tolerance. *Very* gently I said, "Take a deep breath, Ray. I was messin' with you. We're done. No way in the world am I really going into court and tell them you aren't cooperating on the basis of one exercise."

He stood stone still.

"I'm backing away. If you need to take a little time, go ahead outside and walk around a little. Have a cigarette. Come back when you're ready."

No movement.

"Breathe."

I watched his shoulders slowly raise, then drop.

"One more."

Again.

"Wanna take a little break?"

"And let you assholes talk about me? Hell, no." He stalked back to his chair and sat.

"Ray, what'd I do there?"

"Almost got your skinny ass killed."

"Besides that."

He thought a minute, but I could see he was just getting madder. "I don't know what the hell you did. You're so smart, counselor, you tell me."

"I humiliated you. I took the thing you're afraid of and rubbed it in your face."

15

"I wasn't afraid of nothin'. Afraid of what?"

"Not being able to control your temper. Being a bad dad."

"I ain't afraid of any of those things."

"Okay, I took the thing you're *maddest* at and rubbed it in your face." Same thing.

"That's closer."

"Did I teach you any respect?"

He looked at me like I was a booger on his plate.

"It feels exactly the same to your girlfriend's kids. You can get them to say what you want because you're a giant and they know you'll hurt them. But you can't control what they think, so while they're making the apology, what do you think they're thinking? And how mad do you think they're getting?"

"They're kids. They got to learn."

"And what do you think they're going to do someday when they're big enough to act on that anger?"

"Neither one of them little turds ever goin' to be as big as me."

"So they'll take it out on some girl or some kid or some boss." There are a million ways to screw up your life with rage. "Do you see what your temper almost did to you? Cheated you out of the very thing you want. You were just about ready to say 'I don't give a damn,' and take me out, and destroy any chance of getting what you want."

I don't know how much of the Lesson of the Night was lost on Ray, but some of the other guys got it. The lesson for me was simple. Having experienced my own temper over and over, watching myself destroy things I loved and cared about all my life, gave me just enough knowledge to know when to stop, thereby keeping all my body parts attached.

So maybe it's a good thing my mother didn't actually get my temper *cured*. Though it wasn't her intention, she gave me a tool. That apparent contradiction validates something I've come to believe over my adult life: You can't tell the good stuff from the bad stuff when it's happening. In fact, it isn't good or bad. It's just stuff.

Bawlbaby

—◆—◆—◆—

2

UNTIL ABOUT THE AGE OF TWELVE, the best use I found for my temper was to keep me from being a bawl-baby. One of the few things I could do better than almost all my peers was cry. I cried when *anybody* hit me. I cried when I was down to my last—second—cookie; when it was my brother John's turn to ride with my dad or my granddad in the gas truck; when my mother gave the second half of my Popsicle to someone else (that fell into the second-cookie category); when the New York Yankees lost a World Series game; anytime I had to share and anytime someone wouldn't share with me. Any event that could light up my temper could also reduce me to tears. Sometimes there was a choice, but often I just went for both. Physical pain, or the threat of it, could crank me up pretty good, but emotional pain took me *out*. The moment I considered myself either the cause or the focus of disappointment, my eyes would squint, my lips would spread wide over my buckteeth, and it was a race to my chin between tears and snot.

Faced with that, my dad would simply grimace and shake his head, or if he was feeling particularly irritated, ask another of those famous questions to which he didn't want the correct answer: "Do you want me to give you something to cry about?" (No, Crutch, I do not want you to give me something to cry about. I already have something to cry about, thank you. Why don't you give *your* something to cry about to John or Candy?) My mother, on the other hand, when she wasn't suckered in by my dramatic despair, hated it. Her question was more taunting: "What are you going to do now, be a big bawlbaby?" That made it worse because the answer was yes, but the response had to be no. And the river would run.

Shortly after the end of World War II, my father opted out of the army air corps and came to Cascade, my mother's home and birthplace. Stories in my family were told without much emotion, but my imagination says there were wounds to heal. My grandfather Glen had lost his parents at an early age, then lost his son, my mother's brother, in the war. My father lost his own dad in the months just following his return from overseas duty.

The idea of owning his own business appealed to Crutch, and when he gave up his lifelong dream of flying to settle down, he decided to go into the wholesale oil and gas business with Glen. From my earliest memories to the time I was out of college, I'll bet I didn't see my father dressed in anything other than a Mobil Gas or Phillips 66 uniform more than a dozen times. He became the Valley County clerk of the court in the years after I graduated from college, and each time I'd come home I'd barely recognize him in street clothes. At any rate, when he came to be a gas dude, Crutch got a new dad, May and Glen got a new son, two grandsons and a granddaughter, and the pain of loss eased up a little all around.

What all that meant to me is that I would receive a lot of my early lessons staring out the passenger-side window of a gas truck, looking for deer or bear, as my father or Glen drove me into the Idaho backcountry, or sitting on their laps, my hands gripping the steering wheel, believing I was a gas-truck driver. I loved those trips and hated when it wasn't my turn, or worse, when my brother tricked me out of my turn.

As was often the case, it came down to cookies.

I'm five years old, sitting at the kitchen table eating lunch; my older brother, John, is across from me, and my sister, Candy, is locked into her high chair. My granddad is taking a load of gas to Garden Valley in the big truck, and he has invited both my brother and me to go. It is not normally considered a smart idea by the elders in my family to put my brother and me in the same truck for a long trip because, though I have a seriously misguided case of hero-worship, John does not hold me in that same regard and before we're back one of us will be bawling and it will be me. But my grandfather is deemed nicer than he is smart, and today he's taking us both.

I'm so excited I can barely hold water, scarfing down my tomato soup and tuna sandwich, anticipating eating my Oreos frosting first (a frivolous act that would cause immediate loss of those Oreos were my dad present at the table) and then the great ride with my brother and my granddad in the big truck with the flying red horse painted on the tank. For life to get better than this, I would have to wait until the day in the middle of my thirty-seventh year when my agent called and said we had done pulled the wool over the eyes of the Greenwillow Books people and they were going to publish my novel.

My mother opens the package of Oreos and places two each on our plates. My brother watches as I twist the first one open, revealing the cool white frosting, and lick it clean. I eat the chocolate cookie outsides slowly; one more whole cookie to go. That was a *little* fast, I'll slow down on the second one. Even at five years old, I am aware of the need to stretch out my enjoyment.

As I twist the second Oreo, John says, "You want my cookies?"

For a second I think he asked if I wanted his cookies. I lick my frosting, daring not to dream.

"Hey, Chris. You want my cookies?"

I look up. They sit on his plate, untouched. "Yeah! You're not gonna eat 'em?"

"Not if you want them," he says.

I glance over at my mother. She raises her eyebrows and shrugs.

I reach across the table for them (another act that would result in surefire cookie loss if my dad were in the room). John pulls the plate out of my reach. "You gotta let Joe go with me to Garden Valley." Joe Boyd is our next-door neighbor and my brother's best friend.

"What do you mean?"

"Joe's never been on the truck, so I wanted to take him

with me. You can have my cookies if you'll let him go."

I look at my mom again, and she again raises her eyebrows and shrugs, which should be a sign to me, but I'm five years old, for Chrissake, and there are *two extra cookies* in my immediate future. John sees the hesitation in my eyes. "Crutch is going to McCall tomorrow, and it's your turn in the little truck, so you only have to wait one day."

Those Oreos are actually staring from his plate right at me. They can talk. They can sing. *You only have to wait one day . . . you only have to wait one day . . . hi ho the Derry-o, you only have to wait one day.*

"I don't know . . . "

"Joe's never been on the truck," he says again. "Come on." He pushes the cookies toward me.

The cookies twist themselves open, taunting me with the cool creamy frosting. They are getting naked for me.

"You'll get to go tomorrow."

"Boy . . . "

"And next time my turn comes for Tommy Davis's you can have it." Tommy Davis lives about three miles outside of town . . . but the cookies are dancing now, slowly dropping their outer layers. They have frosting underpants.

"Joe really wants to go. He said he'd let you be Roy Rogers the next time we play cowboys." Even *I* know that's a lie; Joe Boyd is known to have beaten people up for playing Roy Rogers even when he wasn't there, but cookies are singing "Happy Trails" to me and suddenly they are in my sweaty little hand. My brother looks at my mom. In the distance, through the sugary cloud that has shrouded my mind, I hear him say, "He touched 'em. He has to eat 'em now. Can I go call Joe?"

Jewell looks at me with pity and nods, and my brother is excused from the lunch table to finish turning my afternoon into hell. But for this moment I'm in Heaven. Extra cookies only happen on birthdays. I take my time with the first one, twisting it slowly, licking each molecule of frosting before nibbling the dark chocolate. Still, it lasts less than a minute. By the time I have cleared the frosting from half of the second cookie, deep depression rolls in. The second cookie of two or the last cookie in the package carries the same sad emotional weight of loss. No more cookies, and Joe Boyd is going to Garden Valley. My mom watches as my eyes squint, my mouth opens, tears squirt, and I don't even finish the second cookie.

She doesn't have to ask *if* I'm going to be a bawlbaby, but *how long* I'm going to be a bawlbaby. I think probably until they get back.

When my granddad comes to pick us up and gets Joe

instead of me, he comes into the house. I'm still sitting at the table blubbering. "Why did you do it?" he asks, ruffling my hair. "Why'd you let your brother trick you?"

I sniff back the tears, convulse a couple of times, and blurt, "Because I like cookies."

Until his death, my granddad would consider that one of my best lines.

My mom threw up her arms. "I knew this would happen," she told him. "He's going to be mad the rest of the afternoon, but maybe it will help him learn."

The capacity to delay gratification came in my thirties.

I think a significant fraction of my personality structure resulted from my father and grandfather working together in the wholesale/retail gas and oil business. Not only did the delivery trips provide great sources for anticipation, but just hanging out down at the service station with the two of them was pretty neat. They were personality opposites, my grandfather an impulsive extrovert, my father more thoughtful and quiet and maddeningly rational.

A beautiful young woman with Ada County (Boise) license plates pulled into the station one day, and my granddad hustled out onto the island to wait on her. Now, I don't know the whole story on my granddad, but I know his preteen and teenage years were spent as an orphan, finding a home in the sheds and outbuildings of relatives, hugely thankful to be allowed to work for food and shelter. In his early twenties he was considered the most helpful man in town; if your truck stalled or was stuck in the hills, call Glen Morris. If your car was out of gas or you didn't have a car and needed a lift in an emergency, call Glen Morris. If you were a stranger traveling through Cascade in the middle of the night and you needed aid of any kind, the night cop would get you in touch with Glen Morris.

I remember one day in late spring when I was about five, walking across the dirt street to my grandparents' house to see the nest of robins atop the wooden pillar holding up the roof of the open-air porch. Glen had pointed them out to me a couple of weeks earlier, and we were even present for the hatching of the eggs. It was hard to see everything over the edge at the top of the pillar, but I was fascinated watching the mother cramming worms halfway down the babies' skinny throats. It made me appreciate the fact that my mother only made me sit at the table until I ate my vegetables.

On this particular day I couldn't see anything over the edge of the pillar no matter how far I stretched, and I finally crawled onto the railing to get a better look. Still no birds, but there was muffled peeping from *inside* the pillar.

When I realized the nest had become a fast elevator down into the hollow of the pillar, I panicked and ran screaming into the house. May was in the backyard hanging up clothes, and Glen stopped eating his Cream of Wheat and toast long enough to calm me down so I could tell him oh no oh no oh no the babies were buried alive and would certainly die a slow miserable death. He brought me back outside, put his ear to the pillar, and smiled. "Easy," he said, and disappeared into the house, returning with a hand jigsaw. He cut a little arched doorway at the base of the pillar, and we peeked in. Sure enough the babies were all there, squawking and appearing as if they actually *wanted* worms. The mother bird returned with one right on cue, flew to the top of the pillar, and seemed for a moment to panic. Glen moved me away from the new archway, and within minutes she discovered it, disappeared inside, and the squawking stopped. My granddad had turned a tomb into a castle in a matter of moments.

He looked at the piece he'd cut out. "Your grandmother isn't going to be happy about this," he said.

"I'll tell her you saved the birds."

"You do that," he said, his expression revealing not one iota of relief.

"You saved the birds," I said again.

"I cut a hole in your grandmother's porch," he said back.

I wasn't present for the conversation they must have had, but Glen prevailed, because the mother bird fed those babies through that golden arch every day until they were ready to venture out. When they were all gone, Glen removed the nest and replaced the missing piece using some kind of wood glue and small nails. You have to look close, but you can see it today.

Because of his lonely upbringing Glen longed for a family, and it was understood that he thought of himself as the luckiest man in the world for hooking up with my grandmother May, and, hole in the porch or no, he lived to serve her. May might have seemed like a sweet southern belle to the townspeople, but she ruled her world based on a rigid sense of right and wrong, and her principal weapon was guilt. My granddad didn't drink, didn't smoke or tell bawdy jokes, and he did his best not to cuss around her, if only to avoid her icy glare.

Let me back up a little further and say that when you're a kid with puberty in the distance, and Ronny Cooper catches you and a couple of your buddies by the swings over at the school playground and delivers the hot poop on human reproduction in terms that would be edited by *Hustler* magazine, your life changes. He speaks of body fluids you know nothing about and predicts that someday you'll be mixing yours with a girl's. He even uses the names of possible candidates. You're embarrassed and even repulsed, but neither as much as you are intrigued. Then he tells you that your parents have done it at least as many times as they have kids, and gets specific about the source and destination of those body fluids. You're almost in a rage, and scream no way not my parents and you'd like to kick his butt, but Ronny Cooper is two years older than you are (though only one grade ahead) and crazier and meaner than an outhouse rat. It is far smarter to let him besmirch the reputations of your naked parents than to tell him he's full of shit. You walk away in complete and utter disbelief, but the truth has a ring of truth to it, and pretty soon you're admitting that no way is Ronny Cooper smart enough to make up something like that, and all of a sudden your mind is filled with very distasteful visions of your parents. If you're intellectually curious, you extrapolate: from your parents to your friends' parents, even to your grandparents. Reluctant as your mind is, it all falls into place.

But not for May Morris. I'm fifty-five as I write this, and I still believe my mother and her brother were products of divine conception, not because their behavior was in any way elevated, but because there is simply no way, even today, that my imagination will wrap around the vision of my grandmother having sex. May Morris was one chilly lady.

So it makes sense that, though my grandfather would *never* stray, he might be quite a flirt with a vivid imagination. He took that imagination with all its flirtatiousness with him onto the island that day to wait on this stunning young woman in her brand-new Buick with the Ada County license plates.

It turns out she didn't have money for gas to put in her brand-new Buick. Either she had lost her purse or it had been stolen, but she was willing to give my grandfather her doorknob-sized engagement ring to hold if he would fill her tank and loan her twenty dollars to get home, where she would promptly put a check in the mail. He was then to send her the ring, but be sure to insure it for at least a thousand dollars, because her fiancé loved her dearly and this was a truly classy piece of jewelry. She then looked sadly and longingly at the ring and started to remove it from her finger. But sadly and longingly were just the ticket with my granddad, and he told her to leave that little jewel right where it was; he could tell by the look in her supple breasts—er, eyes—that she was honest as the day was long. He filled her tank, put an extra five gallons in a can that he placed in her trunk, and pressed the twenty plus another five in her soft, manicured hand; he gave her a stamped envelope with *Morris and Crutcher, Mobil Gas, Cascade, Idaho,* on it, and sent her on her way.

Back in the front office, my dad listened to his story, shook his head, smiled from ear to ear, and asked Glen why he didn't just take that sweet little thing over to Cascade Auto and buy her a brand-new Dodge. "That's twenty-five bucks and the price of a tank of gas you'll never see again," he said.

"You're a good man, Crutch, but obviously not much of a judge of character. That money will be in my pocket by the first of the week."

"Glen, that's the oldest trick in the book."

"*I'm* the oldest trick in the book," Glen said. "Wait and see."

"Wanna make it a little more interesting?" my dad asked.

"I'm down about thirty-three now," Glen said. "That's about as interesting as I can stand."

My dad reached into his pocket and took out a five, slapping it down on the counter. "There's five more says you don't get a penny."

My granddad said, "You're on."

I said to my dad, "I think Glen might win. That lady was really pretty."

"I know she was," Crutch said. "I know she was."

By the first of the week my granddad was doubting if

he'd put a full three-cent stamp on the envelope, and by Wednesday he was cursing the United States Postal Service for making a perfectly decent and beautiful citizen of the U.S. look like a common criminal. My dad gave him until Friday, and on noon of that day, Glen limped across the street on his metal hip to retrieve the mail from our post office box. I'd gone to work with my dad every day that week, just to be there when the money showed up, but the slowness of Glen's stride and the pained look on his face as he limped back across the street said his Marilyn Monroe look-alike had done taken him to the cleaners.

My granddad was resilient, though, and by the middle of the afternoon he was comfortable with the idea that he'd been hoodwinked and was busy concocting a story to tell my grandmother about where thirty-seven dollars might have mysteriously gone.

My dad shook his head again and rubbed the back of his neck with his hand, a gesture I would witness each and every time he caught me in a bonehead move until the day he died. "What were you thinking, Glen? I just can't figure out why you'd fall for that."

My granddad smiled sheepishly, then lit up and said, "I like cookies."

Something Neat
This Way Comes

◆◆◆

3

"WANNA DO SOMETHING NEAT?" are four words
that strike terror in my heart to this day. My answer was
always yes when the question came from my brother. Then
he'd tell me what the neat thing was, and it would always
seem not so neat until he explained how what *seemed* like
something that could really get you in trouble was, in fact,
neat. Then I'd get in trouble.

I'm around six years old and I'm playing cowboys outside with my friend Ron Boyd and some other kids from the
neighborhood. I have to pee so bad I'm about to turn into a
hurled water balloon, but Ron's older brother, Joe, is not

around and we younger kids have sworn that no one will tell him we're playing Roy Rogers, lest we pay dearly, and for the last half hour or so, I've been Roy. If I go inside to pee, I stand to lose my exalted spot atop the yellow broomstick that is Roy's mighty palomino, Trigger, and I'm working my sphincter muscles like a body builder, prolonging those last precious minutes. Finally agony wins out and I drop my cap pistol to get a better grip on my penis and streak for my house. John, sitting in a chair reading a book, observes the obvious as I burst through the door and says, "Wanna do something neat?"

"Yeah, but just a sec. I gotta go to the bathroom."

"That's the neat thing," he says. "Go there." He points to the four-by-five heat-register grate in the middle of the living-room floor.

"Huh-*uh*," I say. "You'll tell."

"Promise I won't," he says. "Wait till you see what happens. It's really neat."

By now I have to go so bad I'm dizzy, and only my death grip is stopping me from peeing into the wall like a strip miner.

"Just take down your pants and pee down the grate," he says. "I promise I won't tell. I'd do it myself, but I don't have to go."

"Have you ever done it before?"

"Lots of times," he says. "And see? I never got in trouble for it."

"No, sir . . ."

"You'll be sorry if you don't. It's really neat."

"Okay, but you *promise* you won't tell."

He crosses his black heart.

In the same nanosecond my pee hits that hot furnace, the yellow steam rolls up around me like I'm Mandrake the Magician in the middle of a disappearing act, which I'm not but *really* wish I was. I know instantly from the *ssssssssss* and the horrific stench that I better not be making plans to play Roy Rogers again soon. I best be rehearsing my role as a jailbird, because it is going to be a *long* time before I leave my room.

This is a job for bawlbaby. My eyes squint and my lips roll back over my buckteeth and not one tear comes out because every drop of water in me is shooting out like I'm trying to arc it across the Grand Canyon.

My brother calmly closes all the windows.

When the last drop sizzles off the top of the hot oil furnace, I stand, gazing dazed through the yellow mist. "You said you wouldn't tell."

"I won't," he says, "but what are you going to tell Jewell and Crutch when they come home and smell this?"

"You better open those windows."

"And let the whole neighborhood smell it? Then you'd *really* be in trouble."

John could always get me to help him pound those last few nails into my coffin for him. He not only got me, he got *me* to get me. I'm running around closing the rest of the windows for him so the neighbors won't form a mob to run my parents out of town for having me as a kid.

True to what I now know my brother already knew, he didn't *have* to tell on me. When Jewell walks through the door carrying my baby sister, the aroma fills Candy's tiny nostrils and sets her off like a siren. Besides, if you're from *Mars*, there's no mistaking that smell. The good news is that Jewell is so mad she doesn't know exactly how she wants to kill me, so I get a short reprieve "until your father gets home."

I can truthfully say I don't ever remember my father hitting me, but somewhere I got the idea he could hit really hard, and I always put that idea together with this particular incident. So if my dad ever warmed my butt, it was in response to my doing something neat onto the oil-furnace fire through the living-room grate. But make no mistake about it: Whether or not my father hit me, it didn't change my behavior one bit. The claustrophobic horror of those first few seconds, and the telling and retelling of the tale, are far more natural consequence than I need to never again pee down the heater. It is good that May and Glen live just across the street, because our house is uninhabitable for at least four days and we have to wait two days after *that* for the curtains to get back from the dry cleaners. But I don't go down totally alone. It is widely believed I am telling the truth when I say John told me to do it ("I was just teasing. Geez, I didn't think he'd really *do* it") but his is a misdemeanor and mine a felony that spawns another of those unanswerable questions I will hear throughout my elementary-school years: "If your brother told you to jump off a bridge, would you do it?"

Of course I would, if he made it seem neat.

There are plenty of wanna-do-something-neat? stories, each more embarrassing than the last, but my brother's real coup had to be the time he shot me in the head with a BB gun and didn't spend one second behind bars for it.

My father would never let any of us kids have a BB gun. "I'll let you have a twenty-two when it's time," he'd say, "but a BB gun is a toy and that makes it dangerous." We would be allowed to own and shoot a real weapon when we were of age for a hunting license and when he was convinced he had taught us the gravity of holding in our hands a weapon that can kill. So how badly do you think each of us longed for a

BB gun? Of course John knew how to get his hands on one.

We had moved into the big house near the beginning of my second-grade year and found new friends in the Young brothers, Eddie and Richie. Their dad, along with his brother, owned Cascade Auto, the place my dad thought my granddad might as well have gone to buy his pretty blond felon a new car. Eddie and Richie Young could unerringly identify any car made within the last fifteen years that drove down Main Street; and they could have shot the windows out of any one of them because they had a Daisy Red Ryder BB gun.

One of many grievous errors I could never convince my parents they were making was that of appointing my brother baby-sitter whenever they left home. Cascade, as I've said, is a small town, and in those days so safe no one even locked the doors to their houses or cars. Nine- and ten-year-olds were routinely left to baby-sit younger siblings, and I am lucky to have lived long enough to say it was a bad idea, at least in the case of John Morris Crutcher. They must have known it wasn't a great idea because they left my sister, Candy, with our grandmother. "You don't know what he's like," I'd tell my parents when they were getting in the car.

"Oh, it can't be that bad, Chris," my mother would say. "You always overdo it."

Oh, yeah?

I'm seven and John is two years and nine months older. No sooner than the dust clears our driveway, he asks, "Wanna do something neat?"

"What?"

"This is something *really* neat."

The yellow steam rolling out of the heat register, forever staining my T-shirt and my reputation, is little more than a distant memory.

"Tell me what it *is*."

"Wait here."

He returns, Eddie Young in tow, packing Eddie's brand-new BB gun.

I've got him now. "You're gonna get in trouble. We're not supposed to have those."

"We're *not* having it. It's Eddie's."

"Yeah, but we're not supposed to even have it around."

"Shut up. Now do you want to do something neat?"

I eye the gun. So forbidden. *So* neat. "I guess. What?"

"You go down and hide behind the tree, then whenever you're ready, run as fast as you can along the ditch and we'll shoot at you."

Our front lawn sprawls over a gently sloping hill clear down to Main Street, the only paved street in town and also

Highway 15, the lone state highway connecting southern and northern Idaho. Thick pine trees stand on the north and south ends of the lawn and a shallow gravel ditch runs its length, next to the highway.

"No, sir. I'm not doing that. What if you hit me in the head?"

He points to the sky. "Look, dummy, it's almost dark. We'll barely be able to see you, much less hit you in the head. It's like the shooting gallery at Zim's. Come on, it'll be neat."

The image of the shooting gallery does it. About forty miles north of Cascade, six miles outside an even smaller town called New Meadows, is Zim's Plunge, a swimming pool fed by natural hot springs. It is open year round, even on the coldest days of a snowy winter, and going there is a truly special treat. No one leaves Zim's without spending a few dimes in its shooting gallery, which consists of a primitive electronic rifle holstered about twenty feet from a small plastic bear behind glass on runners. The bear has an electronic target on both sides and on his stomach, and if the light from the gun hits that target, the bear rises to its hind legs and roars, turns a one-eighty, and heads the other way. Once you get him on his hind legs, you can keep him there by firing into the target on his stomach. He roars and kind of jerks one way and then the other until you miss. No matter how many times you hit him, nothing happens more than a roar and a reversal of direction. He does not drop to the ground like a rock the way I do when the first BB my brother fires hits me square in the temple. Porch lights switch on in all three houses on adjacent blocks as I lie on the ground holding my head, screaming what I know are probably the last sounds I will make. Eddie Young snatches his BB gun and runs for home as my brother races down the hill to my side.

"What's going on over there?" a neighbor hollers. "Chris Crutcher, is that you making all that noise?"

"It's okay!" my brother yells back. "He just fell down. I'll take him in the house."

I scream louder, my temple pulsating. John takes my hand away from my head and feels the spot where the BB hit. There is a small bump. I scream louder. "Shut up!" he says. "I'll get you in the house." The pain isn't all that bad, really. The *thud* of the BB scared me more than it hurt me, but I have him on the ropes, because he has shot me in the head with a BB gun we weren't supposed to have and he is in big trouble now and I can even imagine my parents will from now on make *me* the baby-sitter, should I pull through. I scream even louder.

"You better shut up," he warns. "The BB is in your head and if you keep screaming, it will work its way to your brain."

I suck back my next scream like a black hole.

"Fastest way to get anything to go to your brain," he says, "is loud noise." He picks me up and helps me up the hill.

"Maybe so," I tell him, "but you're really in trouble now. You're gonna get it. I'm tellin'."

"You can if you want," John says, "but if Jewell and Crutch ever find out you have a BB in your head, you're *really* in trouble, way more than me."

"No, sir . . . "

John shrugs. "Don't believe me."

"How am *I* in trouble?"

"They'll want to get it out," he says. "If you just leave it alone it will come out by itself, but you know grown-ups. You'll have to go to the doctor. He'll put you to sleep and cut it out with a knife. A lot of guys don't make it."

Man, this is *no* fair. "Don't worry," he says. "I won't tell."

"Promise?"

"Yeah, well, you know, if you don't make me."

"I won't make you. . . . How would I make you?"

"You know, like being a jerk, or not doin' me favors."

I promise I won't be a jerk and I'll do all the favors he wants if he will please, oh, please not tell Jewell and Crutch I have a BB in my head, so they won't take me to the doctor to have my head knifed open.

My brother extorted late-night glasses of water, extra desserts, and cover-ups until I was nearly in junior high school, all because I had a BB in my head. Instead of a brain. In fact, I didn't have either.

I didn't have the heart to gun down my four-year-old sister in that same ruthless fashion, but a few months later I did talk her into *swallowing* a BB, then coerced favors from her with an altered version of what happens when a BB works its way from your stomach to your heart. My ploy worked until just after breakfast of the next day when Candy, famous for rifling through her stools looking for corn, found the BB.

I told that story to my parents sometime in my late thirties, at another of those Christmas get-togethers, and John, by then a respected Seattle accountant, listened carefully, even smiled in places, and denied it like the older brother he is. He said, "He's a fiction writer, for crying out loud."

Both my parents are gone now; they died without knowing for certain.

Foul Bawl

—◆—◆—

4

WHATEVER DNA COURSED THROUGH my grandfather's veins as he limped out onto the gas pump island to willingly give up more than a day's pay in the name of gallantry coursed through my own veins long before Ronny Cooper gave me the down-and-dirty version of human procreation. From as long ago as I can remember, "perty girls" just turned me on my head. As early as second grade I would sneak off to my bedroom after school so I could "think about perty girls." At nine or ten I could ferret out a hidden *Playboy* magazine—which my father bought because it contained "some of the finest literature published in the country today"—faster than a water witch could zero in on an underground stream. When I opened a current issue to find Stella Stevens buffed out, as they say, only three weeks after I'd seen her mesmerize Li'l Abner in the movie version of the play by the same name, my scalp tingled; my extremities went numb.

Even without Ronny Cooper's or Hugh Hefner's help, I was far ahead of my peers when it came to the gathering and distribution of pertinent information that would turn me into the "go-to guy" of middle elementary school and also get me a semipermanent guest seat in the principal's office. At the beginning of the summer of my tenth year, my father hired me to work cleaning restrooms and dusting shelves and filling the pop and candy machines at his service station, and though it didn't exactly provide me with the training I might later need to climb some corporate ladder, it placed me within earshot of the sexually brilliant high-school kids who pumped gas and lubed cars and fixed flats for him. It was this summer I heard the penis-in-the-pop-corn-bag story that would find its way into my first novel, *Running Loose*, getting me banned like a cult worshiper.

The closer I got to my teenage years, the more I realized that the path to perty girls passed through the locker room. Any way you cut it, jocks got the girls. Cascade sits in the

Rocky Mountain range about eighty miles north of Boise on the winding two-lane that connects southern and northern Idaho. I don't remember a time, then or now, when there were more than a thousand residents. The entire high-school student body numbered barely over a hundred; I graduated with fourteen other students (ten boys and five girls, which may have helped contribute to my social retardation). There was no problem becoming a jock: *Everyone* was a jock; otherwise there weren't enough players to fill a roster. If you didn't show up for football practice on the first day of your freshman year, they simply came and got you. So if you dreamed of something soft and perfumey in your future, you didn't have the same problem outfitting yourself in athletic gear as you might have had in a school of hundreds. Unfortunately, relativity being what it is, it wasn't good enough to get yourself into the uniform, you had to *play*, and it was advantageous if you didn't embarrass yourself doing it. And therein lay the problem.

At the beginning of my freshman year in high school I weighed 123 pounds, with all the muscle definition of a chalk outline. I couldn't complete a push-up. I could run a hundred yards in approximately the amount of time it took me to get a haircut. And I was terrified. My brother, John, was a junior that year, at right around six feet and 230. He started at center on offense and middle linebacker on defense, and he had waited seventeen years to get me into an arena where he and his friends could pummel me without my bawling to my parents. And pummel me they did. I couldn't have bawled to my parents anyway; to bawl you must breathe.

By the middle of the season I was certain I would be granted no audience with any present or future cheerleader or Pep Club member due to football prowess and began looking forward to opportunities in upcoming athletic seasons: basketball or track.

My skills in basketball made me look like Joe Montana in football but the track season brought what turned out to be a defining athletic moment in my tenure as a Cascade Rambler.

I need to back up to say again that I went to high school from 1960 through 1964, a time when there were exactly zero competitive sports for girls. Because I knew some girls who I thought were pretty good athletes, I asked our high-school principal about that. He placed a hand on my shoulder and said, "Chris, you know girls aren't emotionally equipped for competitive athletics." This a day after Jesse Dopler had torn a full set of lockers off the wall because we lost a football game we were supposed to win, Jesse who *was* emotionally equipped.

The girls in our league were offered two interscholastic Play Days per year: one a track meet of sorts in the fall, and the other a round-robin spring softball game. They were allowed no more than three organized practices for each, in order that no school get an advantage over another.

Three track meets into the 1961 season, I have established myself as the only runner in the league who can actually make a track meet longer. Each team is allowed two entries per event with the exception of the mile run, the event in which all "athletes" who don't qualify for any *other* event are dumped. I have not received an official time in any of my first three mile runs because by the time I finish the timers have packed up their stop watches and headed for their cars.

The day my athletic image changes forever, we have just received our new purple-and-gold sweats (gold top, purple pants) and after finishing a set of quarter-mile "sprints" that leave me convulsing on my hands and knees, welcoming an imagined crippling car accident in which I lose my legs and therefore am not required to endure this madness anymore, I pull myself together to stumble for the showers. As I walk over the rise next to the high-school gymnasium, I see the girls in one of their three practices leading to their softball Play Day. At bat is Ellen Breidenbach, a solid, strong girl who appears as if she can hit the ball to Boise. On second base is Paula Whitson, the girl to whom I've been silently pledging my love since first grade. In a school with a population of just over a hundred, it's probably an overstatement to say she doesn't know I exist, but it's no overstatement at all to say, from a romantic standpoint, she doesn't care. As I move closer to the action, I hear Ellen telling the girls she wants to bat but doesn't want to run the bases, and suddenly I understand the meaning of the word "purpose" in the Christian sense. God has placed me exactly here, exactly now, for a purpose. He wants me to get to second base with Paula Whitson.

The girls are getting irritated with Ellen because they want to get on with the game, so I step up and volunteer to run for her. All agree my speed creates no advantage for Ellen but demand that I touch home plate before running to first to keep me from jumping the gun.

I agree, and crouch as close as I dare behind Ellen, a lefty, so I can tag the plate a split second after she hits the ball and be on my way.

The pitcher tosses the ball; Ellen swings for the imaginary fence as I step forward with stars in my eyes to tag the plate. She misses the ball by at least six inches . . . fouls me off.

One of my many missing teeth is stuck in the *bat*.

There are those few seconds following a near-death experience when your body hasn't decided whether or not to send the message of truth to your brain, so it doesn't hurt yet. As I lie on the ground, my brand-new gold sweatshirt now crimson and gold, fairly certain my face has been knocked off my head, I think, This isn't so bad. She has to come see how I am. My imagination pictures a fallen warrior. In the absence of heroics, abject pity will do. I still don't know the extent of the damages, but each girl who leans over to see winces in empathy. In the background Ellen wails, searching desperately for Kleenex. In retrospect, applying Kleenex to what she has done would be like gargling saltwater for a brain tumor.

I gaze into the circle of faces hovering over me; no Paula Whitson. She must have gone for help. Suddenly the girls' heads part for Gary Hirai and Julio Bilbao, two upperclassmen, *real* track guys, who gently lift me to my feet and help me the two blocks to Valley County Hospital. As I glance back, the baseball field is swimming, but I have no problem making out Paula Whitson, slapping her leg with her mitt, waiting for the game to start.

In the days that follow, the story spreads to every corner of elementary, junior high, and high school. Little girls are playing Ellen Breidenbach like I used to play Roy Rogers, empowering themselves by knocking an imaginary Chris Crutcher (whoever *he* is) for a loop. The principal, bless his heart, places the bat, my front tooth still stuck in it like a sharp rock, in the trophy case above the caption DON'T TRY THIS AT HOME, next to a picture of what I used to look like. He is forced to call a moratorium on high-school boys calling out "Strike one!" upon seeing Ellen in the halls, then miming a devastating blow to the mouth and falling to the floor, reducing Ellen to tears each and every time. My dreams of Paula Whitson promising herself to me in exchange for the letter sweater I may never earn are reduced to rubble, so I turn to comedy: removing my brand-new plastic clackers in speech class to deliver an informative speech on "Poithonous Thnakes of the American Thouth" and concocting a ventriloquist's act wherein I place those clackers between slices of a bun and hold a hilarious conversation between Gabby Hayes (Roy Rogers's toothless sidekick) and the world's first talking hamburger. Very high comedy, but not exactly the way to get next to something soft and willing.

In a place like Cascade you simply can't give up on the jock thing, even after you've been reduced to getting ninety percent of your attention with a traveling dental show. The bigger, older guys will finally graduate and you *will* get your chance. So flash forward to the winter of my junior year. I have grown to nearly six feet. My body no longer resembles a stepped-on marshmallow, but rather a strung-out piece of taffy, though there is the shadow of a bump on each arm that may one day grow into biceps; my number of push-ups is nearing double digits. I have put on enough weight to have lettered in football, though certainly not at one of the skill positions, and am allowing my imagination to portray me as a deadeye jump shooter once basketball starts.

Reality, however, says something different. We have thirteen players and twelve uniforms, so I wear JV shorts and a gold T-shirt with the sleeves cut off and the double-0 carefully applied with Magic Marker. If there is a twenty-point differential with less than two minutes remaining in the game, Coach puts me in. Because we have a good team and are never twenty points behind, I always enter a game to wild applause from the home crowd because they know if Coach puts me in, the game is locked. We are exactly halfway through the season—have played each league team once—and I have yet to get a statistic. I do not have a point or a rebound. I do not have an assist. I do not even have a foul. I'm not fast enough to *foul*.

I'm moving through the halls one day when my friend Ron Boyd, football quarterback, high-scoring basketball point guard, turns to me. "Crutcher, we gotta get you some press; it's getting embarrassing to hang around with you."

"Hey, man, at least you get to go home at the end of the day. I have to hang around with me *all* the time."

"Yeah, well, we're going to end all that. We're at McCall this weekend and they suck. We'll be *thirty* points ahead of them when you go in. First out-of-bounds play we get, you haul it down the floor; I'll fire the ball. They'll never expect a fast break with us that far ahead. You'll get two or three shots at the basket before they even know where you are."

I am *pumped*, because though McCall is having a major building year in basketball, they have something any one of us would trade our team for in a heartbeat: Gerry Greene. Gerry Greene is the only girl in the entire league still in the running for the Idaho Junior Miss Pageant. Gerry Greene is tall and dark and heartbreakingly beautiful. If you see Gerry Greene on the streets of McCall, you tell your buddies you had a conversation; if you actually do get close enough to say hi, you tell them you went for a Coke. I know guys with topographical maps of McCall, Idaho, with pushpins stuck in them for Gerry Greene sightings. Gerry Greene is a very big deal. She will be at the game. I am going to score with Gerry Greene.

The game plays out almost exactly as Boyd predicted. With two minutes to go, Cascade leads by thirty-five points.

The other scrubs have been in *twice*. Coach calls me down from the end of the bench. I sprinkle some of the 7 UP I have been drinking on my forehead to look like sweat and untuck my shirt so it will appear as if I'm going *back* in, but the Cascade fans are not to be fooled and take it off the applause meter; McCall is an arch rival. I stand next to Coach as he goes through his substitution ritual: arm over the shoulder, leaning in close, giving instruction. He gives me the same instruction he always gives me— "Don't embarrass yourself"—slaps my butt, and pushes me onto the court.

A McCall player is at the free-throw line, and Boyd meets me at the out-of-bounds line. "If he makes this," he whispers, "go. I'll step out and fire it down. This is your chance."

A jackhammer drills against my sternum as the McCall player sinks both ends of a one-and-one, and I am headed downcourt like a runaway train.

Let it never be said that Chris Crutcher does not listen. My coach's last words before I stepped onto the court were "Don't embarrass yourself." That isn't always easy. At this point in my life I am a deeply religious person, especially when I want something, and I know the Lord works in strange and mysterious ways that make Him sometimes appear as if He's not working at all. I also know He helps those who help themselves, and I'm about to do that, because I have a rap sheet on missed opportunities as long as that of a career felon. If I go down the center of the court, Boyd is going to throw that ball over my shoulder, and, remembering football season, I know my chances of hauling it in are about the same as winning the lottery, which hasn't been invented yet. So I cut down the sideline, thinking I'll hang a one-eighty at the baseline, giving me the best shot at catching the ball.

Like many high-school gymnasiums, McCall's is built at one end of the school, with the inside entrance doors right at the end of that sideline. If I were to keep running straight, I'd run out into the school hall, where the drill team is lined up ready for their postgame performance and where concessions are sold. At least I don't do that.

I'm chugging for the baseline, ready to make my cut. I glance at the electronic scoreboard mounted just above the entrance to see I have plenty of time, get ready to make my cut, glance again at the entrance . . .

. . . and through that entrance walks Gerry Greene. She's carrying a Coke and a hot dog, talking with a friend . . . looking like Stella Stevens.

And I stop. This is a sighting.

My miscue lasts only a few seconds. Somewhere in the back of my consciousness is a roar (which turns out to be the entire Cascade contingent screaming, "Turn around, you jerk!") and I snap to at the same moment the ball *pops!* off the back of my head and straight up into the bleachers. My false teeth spurt out of my mouth like a slap shot and skid to a stop at Gerry Greene's feet. I recognize her expression from back when the Cascade softball players got their first look at my batted-out face. She says, "Ugh" and steps around my teeth. Coach's hand grips the back of my jersey, and I'm scrambling for my teeth because I *know* where I'm spending the final minute of *this* game and do not want to be gumming it.

If you look through past issues of the school newspaper or the *Cascade News*, you will find no record of my participation in the 1962–63 basketball season. I finished with no statistics: not a point or a rebound, not an assist or a foul. But I did declare, and publicly insist to this very day, that on the night of the McCall game in January of 1963, I had a Coke and a hot dog with Gerry Greene.

Of Oysters and Olives and Things That Go Bump in My Shoe

5

JUST AFTER CHRISTMAS VACATION of my senior year in high school, Chuck Steensland, my U.S. Government teacher and the senior-class counselor, caught me in the hall. "Crutcher," he said, "where are you going to school?"

"I'm *in* school."

"I mean college."

"Actually," I said, "I haven't thought a lot about it."

"No time like the present," he said.

I thought I had a lot more time, that you showed up the day college started, like I'd been doing for the past twelve years. I said that.

Steensland took me by the arm. "Allow me to show you our library," he said, in obvious reference to the fact I had avoided that particular room for the past four years like a vampire avoids sunlight. Once inside he introduced me to the librarian, which he thought was pretty funny, and led me to a shelf containing a short row of college catalogs.

"Look through these," he said. "Maybe you'll see something interesting. I'll be over here by the door, to make sure you don't escape." Steensland was a first-year assistant football coach, with arms about the size of my head.

"I'll be right here if you need me," I said.

I noticed most of the catalogs had one thing in common: They were either dark blue and white or black and white. Eastern Washington's was red and white. So I went there.

Little did I know that one well-thought-out decision would set me on the path to my athletic apex, where, among other things, I would be crowned a Stotan. I had tried my hand at competitive swimming during a couple of high-school summers, with pretty much the same degree of success I had experienced in other sports. Paula Whitson's dad had started a small team when someone down in Boise happened to get a look at her almost-perfect stroke and told him she had Olympic potential. When word spread through town that Paula would be swimming, Johnny Weissmuller became my new personal hero and I developed an obsessive crush on the sport. Cascade's pool, fed by hot springs, was nineteen yards, seven inches long, too shallow at one end to flip a turn (even if any of us had known how) with no black line on the bottom to follow. I did not have Paula Whitson's perfect stroke (nor much of her attention) and finished far out of contention each time I actually entered a meet. But Eastern had a fledgling team with too few bodies to swim two relays, and when one of the team members saw me swim from one end of the pool to the other without stopping, he recruited me. It turned out that, with a little coaching and a lot of yards logged, this was my sport.

Actually, my Stotan roots run deep. I didn't even hear the term until I was a junior at Eastern, but when I look back I realize I was chosen from my earliest days.

A Stotan is a cross between a Stoic and a Spartan: simply put, a tough guy who shows no pain. The term was coined by Australian track coach Percy Cerruty in describing Herb Elliot, the world-record holder in the mile run from the late fifties and early sixties. Percy stated in an article for *Sports Illustrated* that Herb was the toughest athlete he'd ever coached; that Herb would routinely run the rest of the Australian national track team into the ground, then tear off his clothes and run over sand dune after sand dune in his single-minded quest to become the best miler in the world and dominate his event in the 1960 Olympics. He did just that. Herb Elliot was a madman.

My college swimming coach happened to pick up that by then ancient *Sports Illustrated* one afternoon in 1966, and by the time we eight unsuspecting mermen wannabes showed for workout, he had translated the Stotan concept from land to water. From the moment I learned about him, I wanted to poke out Herb Elliot's eyes with a sharp, smoldering stick.

We walked onto the pool deck to see, scrawled on the blackboard at the far side of the pool, *Looking for a Few Good Men.* We pretended not to see, but Coach, the G. Gordon Liddy, the Bobby Knight of swim coaches, directed our attention to the fact that he needed volunteers for Stotan Week. We asked what was Stotan Week, and he said show up the first week of Christmas vacation and we'd find out. Oh, no, we said, we don't volunteer for something before we know what it is.

It was ritual to end each workout with twenty twenty-five-yard sprints. On Stotan sign-up day we were up to fifty when, as team captain, I finally gasped, "How many of these are we going to do?"

When there were six names on the Stotan volunteer

sheet over by the table, he thought we might call it a night. Did I mention Coach had recently returned from two years in Army Airborne? The man knew how to get his volunteers.

Eastern Washington State College closed up tighter than a fat man's underpants over Christmas vacation. No dorms, no dinner. No problem. One of our number, Dumbo Banger, the self-described first authentic hippie of EWSC, lived in a condemned apartment above the Beehive Tavern in downtown Cheney, Washington, which he rented for nine dollars a month. The apartment had no electricity save for a single-plug extension cord running out the window, along the side of the building, which plugged in behind the bar downstairs, giving Dumbo access to electricity for one electrical appliance at a time and leaving him in the constant dilemma of choosing light or heat. The only furniture in this palatial suite was a single bed with, crumpled at the foot, sheets that hadn't been washed since the Truman Administration. The true meaning of "hippie," we were to discover, was "unwashed." The day Dumbo moved in, he had purchased a brand-new seat belt from the NAPA auto-parts store across the street and mounted it on the toilet. If you went into the bathroom in Dumbo's place and he didn't hear that familiar click, he pounded on the door until he heard you strap yourself in. Liability, he said, in case you blasted off. The toilet alone got Dumbo a starring role as Lionel Serbousek in my book *Stotan!*

So the rest of us dropped our mattresses out of our seventh-story dorm windows into the back of a borrowed pickup, toted them off to Dumbo's palatial suite, and holed up for Stotan Week, which went like this: Be on the deck in your tank suit at eight o'clock each morning. Work out until noon. Experience *not one minute's* rest. The preferred (read, "required") method for initial entry into the water each day was to march out to the end of the one-meter diving board, execute a military about-face, fold your hands across your stomach, and fall backward, body rigid. Piking your body before entry cost you fifty push-ups. Failing to yell *"Stotan!"* as you fell cost you fifty push-ups. You always volunteered to go first, to avoid the sound of your buddies' backs slapping on the water, increasing your anxiety in anticipation of your own doing the same. Coach wore his black-belted karate *gi* to let us know if we tried to escape he'd simply kick us back into the water. He carried an oversized battery-powered megaphone, through which he delivered all instructions at maximum decibels. If a Stotan were to miss a time standard on a swim or break down during any of the hundreds of drills, Coach would position the bell of the megaphone next to that Stotan's ear and question his gender in very unflattering terms. During intervals in the interval-training swims we were racking off push-ups and sit-ups and dips, or (his favorite) bear-walking—down on all fours—around the twenty-five-foot-square deck, the surface of which was so rough your hands began bleeding after fifteen yards; then out the door, over an eighteen-inch snowbank, around the building, and back in through the opposite door into the ingeniously named Torture Lane, where you sprinted twenty-five yards, pulled yourself out of the pool, racked off ten push-ups, sprinted another twenty-five, racked off another ten, sprinted another twenty-five . . . until he got tired. After bear-walking that far in the snow, your hands felt as if you'd grabbed a fistful of bumblebees when they hit the water.

Our afternoons were spent bundled in sleeping bags on our mattresses in Dumbo's fifty-five-degree apartment, cursing the day Herb Elliot was born and screaming in alphabetical order the names of the STDs we hoped Coach's wife had contracted at the hands of wimpy, sensitive lovers and antiwar protesters.

We survived. Because we hung together, we survived. Nearly twenty years later when I brought my rendition of that time into my book, I did not characterize Coach as Attila the Coach but toned down the description of the training so it would appear choreographed to bring us right to the edge of our potential. Such is fiction. In truth, anyone who allowed himself to go through Stotan Week had earned himself a bona fide mental health diagnosis.

But you don't fall for this Stotan stuff unless you've been groomed for it; Stotans don't materialize out of thin air. There is brainwashing that must occur first, torturous abuse. It was the future Stotan part of me who stood on my pedals, middle finger in rigid salute, cursing the heavens and Bob Gardner as my bicycle sank deeper and deeper into the mud. It was the Stotan part of me who squared off with Jon Probst (who worked with me at my dad's service station) when I was a freshman in high school and he was a junior, two years older, thirty pounds heavier and infinitely stronger, for a one-for-one shoulder punch-out. The object was to make the other guy quit. I'd punch his shoulder as hard as I could, leaving my arm numb from wrist to elbow. He'd smile and punch my shoulder so hard I got whiplash. I'd smile and punch him again. His next one would move me over six inches, and I'd ask if that was *really* all the harder he could hit and unload on him one more time. My punches were little more than an annoyance; his were realigning my skeleton. But in the end he'd stop because if he hit me one more time he'd have to find a place to hide my body. He'd go back to work and I'd go clean the restrooms, careful not to come out until there was no more evidence of tears.

I had learned back in sixth grade there is more than one way to be tough. By then I had been working at my dad's service station for almost two years, and the fact that I had found the key to the candy-bar machine was making itself evident in my body design, which was fast beginning to resemble a pink marshmallow Christmas tree. Narrow at the shoulders and broad at the hip, still waiting for my first real muscle, I might as well have just inserted those candy bars under the skin around my waist like a camouflaged money belt. You could call me many things, but rugged wasn't one of them. Enter Mr. Sandy Tarter, sixth-grade concentration-camp warden.

Up until sixth grade, I had a clean record, if you exclude the day in fifth grade when I asked the teacher why the skin under her arms jiggled so much when she wrote on the chalkboard. (Interesting how, after that, she began locking her elbow to her side while she wrote on the board.)

Mr. Tarter was my class's first male teacher. That could have been a good thing, but Tarter wasn't just any male. Calling Sandy Tarter a no-nonsense kind of guy would be like calling our current differences with Al Qaeda a slight misunderstanding. Tarter was the reverend down at the Valley Bible Center, an Old Testament kind of dude who believed in original sin, which meant you had already done the bad thing for which you should be punished with swift and sure precision. For Tarter, the rod not to be spared was the three-foot, ten-hole hardwood paddle with the beveled edges hanging in the principal's office, and he'd bring it in contact with your butt cheeks at the slightest provocation. In a classroom discussion about our home lives one day, Gene Hamlin said his mother spanked him and his brother every morning because she knew they didn't have it in them to go through the day performing a deserving deed, and Tarter said, "Your mother is an astute woman, Mr. Hamlin. I suggest you ask her to join the P.T.A. and spread the word to some other mothers in this town who may be a little lax, judging from their children's behavior." He paused and scanned the room. "You know who you are."

If you were to commit the misdemeanor of speaking out of turn in Tarter's class, he would likely as not order you to stand in front of the class, arms at a ninety-degree angle to your body, palms up (kind of a crucifixion position, minus the cross) until he said you could put them down. If you complained or if the original crime was closer to a felony, say passing a note or chewing gum or sneaking a SweeTART from your front pocket to your mouth just as you pretended to cough, he would place a book in each of those outstretched arms. If you complained further, he added books. (No wonder I didn't like books.)

What I liked about Tarter was his capacity to reduce us all to bawlbabies, making me decidedly more comfortable with my peers. He is the example I use to this day when pointing out the constitutional wisdom of separation of church and state. Up until the day before Easter break, my punishments in the crucifixion position had always been with other kids, so the humiliation factor was diminished by numbers. But on that day I committed some solo crime and was asked (read, "commanded") to stand before my classmates at the front of the room alone, arms extended.

In the fully developed emotionally healthy human being, the concept "There but for the grace of God" is one that invites compassion: observing that person caught doing what you didn't get caught doing and offering silent support. In the fully developed eleven- or twelve-year-old, who is at best a forty-percent-developed human being, that concept is translated into "There but for the grace of God . . . Ha! Ha! Ha!" A titter ran through the classroom, stifled when Tarter shot his you-want-to-be-next? look across the room. Patsy Cantrell and Bonnie Heavrin, ranch girls who were known to bet on *anything*, passed a note back and forth which, I was sure contained their estimates of how long I would last, plus the amount of the wager. Neither was Paula Whitson to me, but Bonnie was beginning to develop breasts, transforming her automatically into someone you didn't want laughing at you.

I decided my class was about to witness ruggedness in the form of tenacity heretofore unimagined. I fixed my eyes on a spot above their heads, extended my arms as if I were suffering the children to come unto me, and dug in. I sang the lyrics to "Hang Down Your Head, Tom Dooley" in my head, called up what I could remember of *Horton Hatches the Egg*. I tried to recite the alphabet backward, getting all the way to X. Rivulets of perspiration followed one another down the cottage cheese of my torso, slowing at the love handles, then speeding up again to soak into the elastic of my undershorts. Darkness moved in from the sides. I stared directly into Bonnie Heavrin's eyes, taunting myself with the threat of humiliation. I stared at her chest. She made a fist and I closed my eyes.

A traumatic ordeal that seemed to last a lifetime was actually over in a little more than seventy seconds. My hands weighed my arms down like anvils. "Get them up!" Tarter demanded. I pushed with all my might, but my shoulders burned and gave out as my hands sank involuntarily to my sides. Bonnie looked at her watch and passed Patsy a dime. Tarter looked at his watch and shook his head in disgust. "You owe me a recess." Back at my desk I stuck my nose in my social studies book, pretending to give a shit about the industrial revolution to avoid absorbing the humiliating hits from classmates I would gladly have humiliated had they been in my shoes. Silently I congratulated myself. Seventy seconds was by twelve seconds my personal best.

Tarter may have unwittingly given me my first push toward Stotanism, but what prepared me best was undoubtedly my high-school C Club initiation. Jocks from Cascade High School have migrated far and wide over the years, some as far as Garden Valley and Horseshoe Bend to the South, and North all the way to Riggins and Grangeville, and we make our livings at wildly diverse minimum-wage jobs, but what *all* of us have in common is a colossal distaste for oysters and olives. That is not a coincidence.

Often when I'm talking with groups of students in high or middle schools, I imagine they're expecting me to recount how far I had to walk to school through ten-foot snowdrifts with fifty pounds of books, wearing nothing but flip-flops, uphill both ways; those things the geezers of my generation used to tell *me* about. When I started writing books about teenagers, I was thirty-five and needed to bridge only one generation to connect my adolescence with theirs. Now it's two. What I say and believe is that humans of any generation are far more similar than we are different. True, if you were a drug abuser in Cascade, Idaho, in 1964, you'd pretty much have to do it with a case of beer; and if someone brought a gun to school, it was because he went hunting in the early morning and left the gun in the gun rack of his pickup, which disturbed no one because there were three or four other pickups in the parking lot similarly armed, and the thought of bringing those weapons inside to take care of business simply didn't exist.

An event of less than life-changing proportions might take two or three days to make the evening news (which lasted fifteen minutes), if it made it on at all. No Internet: The information highway was a single-lane logging road winding through steep mountains, dead-ending at some nameless "crick." But all teens, then and now, are *becoming*, and that is the connector. We're watching and considering and wondering what happens next; finding our places in the universe; entertaining beliefs that will become guideposts for our thoughts and actions for the rest of our lives. I rely on mutual agreement on that concept to boost my credibility when I'm standing before a group of teenagers.

Which is why I *never* tell them about C Club initiation. They would say, "Die, old man! We are not the *least* bit similar. We are not the same species. Spock, are you out of your Vulcan mind?"

See, earning an athletic letter at Cascade High School was a mixed blessing. To become a full-fledged letterman with all the rights and privileges thereof, you were required not only to letter but to join the C Club, which meant you must go through C Club initiation, after which you were eligible to pick a girl from the top row, though it didn't guarantee you'd be on the top row when the eligible girls did their picking. Always an element of risk.

To put the entire C Club experience into perspective, I need you to understand that the C Club sponsored *one* activity during the entire school year: a shotgun raffle. (Speaking of our similarities and differences, *you* show up at school with a plastic pistol no bigger than your fingernail from your old G.I. Joe set and get three days out-of-school suspension and a three-hundred-dollar psychological evaluation. My C Club raffled off a *shotgun* and handed it over to the winner *in school, during school hours*.) The income generated from ticket sales went into the price of next year's shotgun. That's it. Thank you, C Club, for making Cascade High School and the world a safer and better place. So while we didn't have to do anything more than sell raffle tickets to our parents and siblings and extended families to *be* in the C Club, what we had to do to *get* into the C Club would earn a whole bunch of people—starting with the principal and the C Club faculty adviser—thirty years to life if it happened today.

The initiation was shrouded in secrecy, but stories about it leaked like stories out of the Clinton White House, which wasn't invented yet. They couldn't be true, they just *couldn't* be true.

They were true.

Each initiate was required to make a hardwood paddle, three-feet long with ten holes and beveled edges, an exact replica of the paddle hanging in the principal's office. That is equivalent to requiring the condemned man to supply rifles for the firing squad and polish the stocks. The best of the paddles, as judged by the school principal, would hang in the office, ready for use by the likes of Tarter and the myriad others who shared his mindset, for the remainder of the year.

As an initiate you spent initiation day wearing your clothes inside out and backward, underpants on the outside. Tight fit. You ran errands for lettermen and the girls they wanted to impress, carrying their books, addressing them as royalty. At the end of the day the student body was called into the gymnasium so the lettermen could run you through more humiliating exercises, singing dumb songs, proposing to unsuspecting girls, playing Cuckoo—in which one initiate would kneel on top of a table with a wet, knotted towel and another would kneel underneath. Both were blindfolded. The one on the bottom was to stick his head out and yell, "Cuckoo! Cuckoo!" and the guy on top would swing the towel at the sound. If the guy on top missed, meet Mr. Hardwood Paddle. If the guy on the bottom got hit, meet Mr. Hardwood Paddle. Us Ramblers knew how to have fun.

In truth we actually welcomed this part of the festivities, because we had at least an inkling of what was to come when the sun went down. At the end of the school day, Ron Hall, the C Club president, gathered us together to instruct us to be at the gym at seven o'clock sharp, and be sure to take a *good* shower.

If your local library advertises my presence at Live at the Library and I don't show, it's because I've disappeared into the Witness Protection program, since as we entered the gymnasium that evening, we each signed an oath never to reveal the specifics of the upcoming event. They didn't threaten death and dismemberment (not necessarily in that order) for anyone breaking this oath; they *promised* it.

———◆◇◆———

The gym doors slam shut. I have been dreading this since sixth grade, when I first heard the high-school kids at my dad's service station talking about it. I have particularly dreaded it since the beginning of this year, because I finally won a starting position on the football team, which meant there was no way around it. Some of my classmates lettered as sophomores; they get to deliver the torment, adding to my humiliation.

We leave our clothes in our lockers, stand naked in a line while President Hall reminds us of the sanctity of the event; when we walk out of here, we'll be men. Several mason jars filled with gray, oversized, slimy oysters sit on a table by the stage. The lettermen remove them from the jars, handing us one each. They're slick, they tell us, they'll go down easy. The paddles are cocked behind our bare butts. Just swallow those babies right down. But wait! These are awfully expensive oysters, they might want them back. They tie strings around one end of each oyster, wait till we swallow, then *pull them back*.

As anyone who has ever undergone any procedure whose name ends in -oscopy knows, the Master of the Universe did a marvelous job engineering the human body. There are bones and muscles by the score we don't even notice most of the time, until we try to use them in some way for which they're not designed. Like BACKWARD!!! Raw oysters are bad enough, but raw oysters on the way back up tickle the very edges of the imagination.

You couldn't send a Mars probe to the edges of my imagination from where we go next: the Olive Race.

Seven naked letterboys line up across one end of the gym on their hands and knees next to seven naked letterboys' *shoes*, staring downcourt at seven black, unpitted olives. At the sound of the cap pistol, we crawl to the other end, *sit on the olives and pick them up!!!!!!!!!!*, stand and run, cheeks tight, back the length of the gym, to drop the olives into the shoes.

And the last guy has to eat one of the olives, selected at random.

Up until this point in my life I have choked a number of times in spectacular fashion, from the Fourth of July bike race to kissing a baseball bat in lieu of kissing Paula Whitson, but if I choke now I choke twice, once in the race and once on the olive, and thanks to my grandfather Glen and my mother, I'm running dead last.

Neither my grandfather nor my mother has a butt, and their posterioral DNA ran straight down the generational pike to me. To put it crudely: For those of us in that strain of the family, our butt cracks are simply the vortex of our legs. There is none of the cushy excess essential to picking up an olive. I watch in dismay as one after another olive disappears into these lard asses, and I'm getting almost zero purchase. I'm half the basketball court behind when I finally get a good grip and begin waddling toward my shoe, watching my conquerors squat carefully and drop those little black nuggets one by one into their waiting footwear. Only Leonard Irwin hasn't finished, and he's squatting as I cross the free-throw line. He releases as I reach my shoe and smiles up at me as if to say, "Crutcher, you poor buttless bastard." Only there is a God and He is a wrathful God and Leonard Irwin has done something *way* worse in his life than I have, because Leonard Irwin *misses his shoe.*

My father was a World War II B-17 bomber pilot, noted for requiring pinpoint accuracy from his bombardier, and some of *that* DNA must have also come my way down the pike. For once someone else can be the bawlbaby, because I hear that olive drop directly onto the inside heel of my Chuck Taylor Converse All Star tennis shoe and roll toward the toe, and I know Leonard Irwin, and not I, has a one-way ticket for Gag City.

The rest of the initiation consists of events that, were I to describe them, could keep me high on the banned-books list for years to come. Suffice it to say that we learn two new games, Choo-Choo I and Choo-Choo II, and another very inventive activity involving a bucket of bolts, a string, and an appendage that is not an arm or a leg. By the end of the festivities, I have only budding tufts of hair on my head (having visited the C Club barber shop) and budding blisters on my butt. The final humiliation includes the substitution of Tabasco sauce for Preparation H.

When we are showered and back in our street clothes, we sit in the bleachers, strangely euphoric for having survived. President Hall again brings out our signed confidentiality oaths and impresses upon us the importance of keeping this sacred coming-of-age ritual private.

That was 1962. I believe I am the first to squeal.

◆◀◆▶◆

E Equals MC Squared

—◆◈◆—
6

IN THIRD GRADE I TOLD MY classmates that our coal furnace wasn't hot, that you could crawl inside when it was burning full blast and freeze. Because I wouldn't give it up, I got a bloody nose and a trip to the office, where they stuffed cotton into my nostrils and asked where I'd gotten such an interesting notion. It wasn't a notion, I said back, ready to defend my truth if need be; my dad told me.

My dad was a guy you *believed*. He was nearly six feet, five inches tall and weighed around 230. His I.Q. was once measured at 180, though he was quick to say that was an inaccurate measurement because he had read so much more science and history than most kids his age before he took the test. In my later years, looking back, I note he was as quick to tell me it had been measured at 180 as he was to say the measurement was inaccurate.

My dad's mom used to tell us how he'd come home one day in the sixth grade and said to her, "A lot of the other kids in my class think I'm arrogant." She told him there might be some things he could do to change that.

"Like what?" he asked.

"Like giving the other kids a chance to answer questions in class. Like not always having to be right. Like not being the only person to know every little detailed rule to every game you play."

My dad thought a few seconds and said, "Naw, I'd rather be arrogant."

The note I took home from school the day I had challenged my classmates' notions of temperature was addressed to Crutch and not my mom. It came directly from the principal. *Chris got a bloody nose at school today because he told several of his playmates he could crawl inside your furnace and be cool. I'm assuming he got the same lesson on relativity that we get from you on occasion at school board meetings. Please straighten him out.*

I came by that preposterous notion honestly. I had been

in the basement, watching my dad remove clinkers from the roaring coal furnace. Clinkers are the hardened ash residue left when the burnable part of the coal is used, extracted with a set of five-foot tongs. I was fascinated, staring through the open furnace door into the fire, made white hot by the blowing furnace fan. I asked if he thought it was as hot as Hell, where people go to burn forever if they killed someone or took the Lord's name in vain. Crutch didn't believe in a literal Hell but told me if I could go feel the heat of the sun, come back, and jump into that furnace, it would actually seem cold. In fact, it would seem freezing.

He looked up now from the note. "How's the nose?"

"Okay."

"You know you can't get into the furnace, right?"

"You said—"

"I said *if* you could go to the sun and feel the heat. If you could just *feel* the temperature, and then *if* you could come back and get into the furnace, if you could just *feel* the temperature, this fire would seem cold. It would feel cold because the sun is so hot."

"So no way I could ever get into the furnace, even if I could of gone to the sun?"

"No, you would burn up from the heat *way* before you got to the sun." He watched the look on my face as my imagination raced me toward the sun. "You'd melt," he said. "You know, there are some conversations we should probably keep at home. What do you think?"

"How do I know which ones?"

"Well, if you're even close to getting a bloody nose, that's one of the conversations." Not long after receiving that note, my father took to introducing me as Lever. Nature's simplest tool. My sister was quite taken with that moniker. She calls me that to this day.

The school principal wanted my dad to stop giving me lessons my mind wasn't old enough to wrap around, but that was never to be. He just looked for simpler situations. In early December of that same year, he and Taylor Bowlden loaded my brother and me into the back of our jeep to hunt down a Christmas tree. In those days no red-blooded Idaho male would be caught dead buying a Christmas tree from a pile in front of a store, or even cutting one from a Christmas-tree farm, which, if it was invented yet, certainly hadn't worked its way to our part of the country. If you were under the age of eighty-five and had a fake tree, you could legally be cut up for Christmas decorations. The jeep was an army model with a canvas top over the cab and an open back. Neither my father nor Taylor Bowlden subscribed to the notion that children should be coddled, kept warm and safe. They subscribed to the notion that adults get the goodies because they've been alive longer. So my brother and I sat in the freezing open back of the jeep while they sat in the covered cab with a heater and a small flask of whiskey.

We lived in the Rocky Mountains. There were trees two blocks from my house that could have stood in nicely as Christmas trees in a pinch, but hunting for the perfect tree was like hunting for the perfect five-point buck elk, only you didn't have to shoot it. The farther you drove to get it, the more of a fer-real Christmas dude you were, and we spent from eleven Sunday morning until four thirty Sunday afternoon tracking the elusive perfect tree. By the time we arrived back home, my *colon* was frozen and my hands were numb as bricks. I was shaking so hard my voice sounded like I'd swallowed a vibrator. Taylor Bowlden watched us from the toasty cab as we jumped out of the back of the jeep and stumbled into the house on numb feet and said, "That'll toughen those youngsters up." Taylor Bowlden would have been the recipient of the same one-finger salute Bob Gardner got back on that fateful Fourth of July, but I'd have had to break the rest of my fingers off to deliver it.

I ran into the bathroom and began running hot water into the sink. Crutch passed in the outside hall and saw the steam rising, stepped in, and stopped me a split second before I could plunge my icy fingers in. He drained the sink and ran cold water. My eyes widened like a window thrown open on a sunny day, and up popped bawlbaby. I had seen my father as insensitive but never as a brutal torturer. "They're already cold!" I screamed at him.

My sister saw what he was about to do and went screaming for our mother.

"Remember when I told you about the sun and the furnace?"

"Yeah."

"Well, this is that same lesson."

"I got a bloody nose."

"Not from me you didn't. I will guarantee you, young man, that if you stick your hands into hot water when they're that cold, you're going to be crying a lot harder than you're crying right now."

I had long ago sharpened my radar for the term "young man." More often than not it prefaced or followed a warning, but under every circumstance it signified truth.

He eased my hands into the cold water. I swear to God I thought he was a magician. I had watched him refill that sink with freezing water, yet it warmed my hands like the kind of mittens they should obviously have bought me before dragging me into the freezing winter to go hunt

Christmas trees from the back of a jeep.

"Nothing's really cold or hot," he said. "It's all about the temperature of your hands compared to the temperature of the water. Everything's relative."

When the letter from the principal arrived, asking him to explain to me that the water that came out of the cold tap in our sink really was cold and that I had barely escaped another nosebleed defending the antithesis to that, he resumed introducing me as Lever.

My dad's problem was simply impatience with child development. The next time that lesson presented itself, I had relativity down cold.

Everyone in our high school looked forward to their Senior Sneak. It wasn't really a sneak, because the administration knew about it in advance and even provided buses and chaperones. Seniors got a day and a half off from school, which, coupled with a weekend, allowed three days and three blissful nights at the Bar D Dude Ranch outside Pendleton, Oregon. The boys came back with stories of sexual conquests in the bunkhouse, in the rowboat, on horseback, and in the baggage compartment of the bus on the return trip. The girls came home with stories of elbowing the boys in the side of the head as they attempted to grope them in the bunkhouse, in the rowboat, on their horses; stories they must certainly have later filed under the comprehensive title "Boys/Men Are Pigs."

It was traditional for the juniors to try to prevent the Sneak, but usually the seniors left suddenly under the cloak of a fire drill or late at night, and in recorded memory no one could remember the seniors even being slowed down. By my junior year I knew I was without the requisite talents to make myself remembered and revered at Cascade High in any of the conventional, acceptable ways, so the Sneak presented the kind of challenge that made my teeth itch.

I began searching for ways to disable the bus. Though I had worked at my father's service station since the age of nine, my automotive prowess included little more than the ability to fill a vehicle with gas, check the oil, water, and fan belt, fix flats, lube, and change the oil. I also had just enough common sense to know that if I caused physical harm to that bus, our principal, Mr. Evans, would break at least two of his hardwood paddles over my butt.

I suppose I could blame my father; in fact, he's not alive anymore, so I will. It was he who told me that one of his college buddies had spread Limburger cheese on the manifold of Crutch's car right before he and my mother took off on their honeymoon. They drove more than three hundred miles with the windows rolled down, every bit as cold as I'd been in the back of that jeep, and delaying the evening's festivities two or three hours while they huddled in bed thawing out their hormones. If a little Limburger cheese in the right place could slow the adrenaline flow of two virginal honeymooners (hey, they were my *parents*) for a couple of hours, a *lot* of Limburger cheese should slow down a classroom of seniors headed off to create new Rambler sexual myths.

I purchased the cheese from a local pusher sworn to silence and placed it in a locked room behind the furnace where you could freeze if you crawled in, but where Limburger cheese could slowly warm to a moldy stench over the month and a half before the Sneak was to take place. I brought a couple of other classmates in on my plan, and we began scheming to get the putrid cargo aboard the right bus at precisely the right moment. There were three to choose from: two newer thirty-passenger buses and an older forty-five-passenger one. We ruled out the big one because there were only thirteen seniors and the school would need that one to transport grade schoolers. The other two were identical, so we simply needed to keep our eyes and ears open for clues.

About a week and a half before D-Day, one of those buddies, Rick Calendar, a tall, gangly blond kid I'd known since before first grade, called me out of the room during study hall and handed me a small, clear vial half-filled with a pea-soup-looking substance.

I took the vial. "What is it?"

"Smell it."

His expression told me that was a bad idea.

"What is it?

"*Smell* it."

I carefully unscrewed the cap, put it to my nose, and nearly snapped my head off my spine pulling away. If that smell were an explosive, it would be an atomic bomb, a hydrogen bomb, and a cobalt bomb strapped together and detonated over a puppy farm.

Calendar smiled. "Mink scent," he said. "Boy mink gets a whiff of that and starts combing his fur and preening his whiskers. Time to get *frisky*."

I wasn't aware mink wore gas masks to have sex.

There was an invitational track meet down in Boise, a good two-and-a-half hours away by school bus, the night before the seniors were to take off, and we got back to Cascade around midnight. Our intelligence told us they'd be leaving early, before any service stations opened, so we were sure they wouldn't be using the track bus. That left the other small bus as the target of our olfactory ambush. Larry Logue, the third accomplice, attempted to hide in the school shop where the buses were parked, but Coach herded everyone out before he locked it up tight.

I slept fitfully on the couch, rose at about two, and descended to the furnace room. Even with the cheese in a closed container the entire room reeked, and my stomach turned over as I hustled back up the stairs toward fresh air.

It took forever to get into the shop where the targeted bus was parked. All doors were locked tight, and in the end we had to boost Calendar to a high window ledge so he could reach through a hole that had been broken out by a baseball. We were a good two hours behind schedule when that was finally accomplished. Our plan had been to put a dab of mink scent into each of several small plastic pill cups, unscrew the heat vents, and place the cups carefully inside, but we were now painfully short on time, and as a dim glow spread across the eastern horizon we knew we were only a few minutes from the seniors showing and giving us a mink-scent lunch, so we simply poured it through the grates of the side heater vents, spread the Limburger cheese around under the dashboard, and choking and gagging and holding our breath, ran way faster than any of us had run during the track meet the night before.

Fifteen minutes later we watched from a safe distance from behind a parked pickup across the street as the seniors showed up ready for their myth-making trip to the Bar D, boarded with the most titillating of sexual hopes, and streamed off that bus like lemmings. It was four hours before a service station opened so they could gas and service the other bus, and though we didn't stop the Sneak, we gave it a significant delay—a victory for the class Principal Evans had, on more than one occasion, called a "nothing" class.

And here's the lesson in relativity. In the stifling, musky atmosphere of mink scent, a whiff of putrid, three-month-old Limburger cheese smelled like the sweetest of perfumes. The furnace isn't hot, if you go to the sun first. Freezing cold tap water isn't cold, if your hands have been subjected to the bitter elements for five hours ahead of time. And moldy warm Limburger cheese doesn't smell bad at all in the presence of a dark green potion from Hell.

Let me tell you what was bad, and I don't have a relative point to make this good: Principal Evans's reaction after he had to drive that bus three blocks to the Texaco service station to have it reamed out. (You will notice he did not drive it to Morris and Crutcher's Phillips 66 service station, and don't think I didn't consider that. Had we had the school contract that year, I certainly would have thought of a better place to dump my mink scent, because bringing that bus into my own arena would have brought new meaning to the term "friendly fire.")

When Evans finally was able to speak of this incident rationally, somewhere around our tenth reunion, he told us how he drove the bus a block at a time with his head out the driver's-side window, stopping three times to run off the bus and gasp for the kind of air that wouldn't enflame a young buck mink into running down the road after him, hoping to get lucky.

Once again I became famous, for being the ringleader of the group that ended Senior Sneaks for the Cascade Ramblers once and forever; a bit of an overreaction, I thought, on Mr. Evans's part, but of course I didn't have to drive the bus. (The following year, through much charm and groveling, we were able to talk him into "one more last chance.")

In the end, the lesson taught me in the physical world by my father and Limburger cheese and mink scent extended into virtually every corner of my universe and made it possible for me to work in, and tell stories about, a world where searing pain and mind-numbing heroism flow side by side. They intermix and overlap, guiding me away from black-and-white judgments that might come back to haunt and humble me. No one is pretty; no one is ugly. There is no Jesus without

Judas, no Martin Luther King, Jr., without the Klan; no Ali without Joe Frazier; no freedom without tyranny. No wisdom exists that does not include perspective. Relativity is the greatest gift.

The Roots of Angus

7

IN THE FALL OF MY FRESHMAN YEAR, I orchestrated the election of Janice Winthrop as our candidate for Cascade High School carnival queen. Somehow my fourteen-year-old sense of humor accommodated the hilarity of our least popular girl representing our class at the carnival dance. (The carnival queen was chosen differently from other high-school royalty, such as the White Christmas Ball king or the prom queen. After the candidates were elected by their respective classes, their pictures were placed atop compartmentalized shoe boxes, which were distributed to the front office at school and to the downtown merchants.

One vote cost a penny, and people could vote as many times as they wanted by simply dropping money into the slot below the picture of the candidate of their choice.)

Were someone to ask later if I knew it was a rotten trick, I'd have had to plead guilty, because I was smart enough from the start not to want my signature on it. In study hall on the day we were to elect our candidates, I revealed my scheme to a few of my male classmates, at least two of whom would later become embroiled in the mink-scent scandal. Our fall guy was Jackie Craig, whom I goaded in front of the rest of the conspirators into actually making the nomination. Then we put out the word. The class was small; we needed only eight or nine votes, fewer if we could get some abstentions. Janice Winthrop won with five, and at the conclusion of our class meeting that day, we congratulated one another on our comic genius.

Janice was not only considered homely, she was also considered a pain in the butt. She had stringy, mousy brown hair and an elongated face that invited the nickname Horseface, and she was easily ignited. Elton Haskins was once taunting her quietly from the desk directly behind her and she leaped up and started tearing out his hair and screaming at the top of her lungs. No one ever discovered exactly what he'd been saying (Elton claimed he was just asking to borrow a pencil), but that story was told and retold as testament to the fact that she could go off at any minute. In sixth grade Duane Johnston had lured Janice into his garage with the promise of being her boyfriend, stripped her naked, and talked her into some version of what the sixth-grade Duane Johnston considered having sex. He had made more than five dollars that afternoon selling admission to the garage rafters to eight or nine of our classmates. Someone in those cheap seats couldn't keep from bursting out in a guffaw in the middle of the event, and Janice grabbed her clothes and ran nearly naked into the alley, sobbing and screaming at us. Duane came to instant fame. We told everyone Janice was crazy.

The morning after the election, a large sign was posted on the bulletin board at the head of the stairs just inside the entrance to the school: ALL FRESHMAN BOYS REPORT TO THE TEACHERS' LOUNGE BEFORE FIRST PERIOD. DO NOT MAKE THE MISTAKE OF FAILING TO APPEAR. It was signed by our class adviser, Mr. Payne. That would be Mr. LeRoy Payne, better known as Mr. LeRoy Pain.

We had teachers at Cascade High School who could write nearly well enough to be published; we had teachers who could shoot the eyes out of the basket from what would now be NBA three-point land; we had a teacher showing paintings in an art gallery in Boise. We had a teacher who could play the piano or the clarinet well enough to turn professional. Mr. LeRoy Pain could play the ten-hole beveled paddle in the office like some kind of hardwood maestro. He couldn't have been five feet, nine inches tall, and I doubt he weighed 150, but he had wrist action that lifted you a good six inches off the ground with only a half swing. Once, when a rumor sprang up that the Hell's Angels were to pass through Cascade on their way to a motorcycle-gang gathering in Boise, Payne sat in a kitchen chair with a shotgun on his lap out on his lawn just off Main Street and threatened to "pick them off" as they passed through. He was a thirty-year-old ex-juvenile delinquent with a D.A. haircut (ask someone over fifty what the D.A. stands for), whose sense of humor and temper were equally quick.

Suffice it to say Payne didn't bring his sense of humor with him to the teachers' lounge the morning after Janice had become our class royalty. One by one we knocked on the teachers' lounge door, entered, and gazed around the small, dark, smoke-filled room. It was the only time any of us saw the inside of the teachers' lounge, before or since.

"Have a seat, gentlemen," he said. "And I use the term loosely."

We sat. At the uneasy murmur, Payne said, "There will be no talking."

We sat there like the Hell's Angels might have had they actually dared ride through our small mountain logging town in which LeRoy Pain had suspended all civil rights.

Payne brought out a baseball cap from a shelf above the coffee percolator and held it upside down just above eye level. "There are slips of paper with numbers from one to eight in here," he said. "Each of you will draw a number. Number One will ask Janice Winthrop to the carnival dance *before this school day is out*. The rest of you will dance with Janice at least three times that evening. I will be there as a chaperone for no other reason than to count. You do not want to be the guy who dances with her twice. Are there any questions?"

Danny Zimmerman raised his hand.

"I said there would be no talking," Payne said.

Danny Zimmerman put his hand down.

"Good." He passed the hat around; each of us drew a number. The same God who turned His back on Leonard Irwin during the Olive Race now turned His back on Gene Gestrin, who hadn't even been present for the vote. When someone found the courage to bring that up, at our fifteen-year class reunion, Payne said, "The emperor of Japan wasn't at Pearl Harbor, either, but I still hold him responsible." For the first time since it had happened, he smiled about the subject. "I wasn't about to get into an argument with any of you guys about who may or may not have masterminded it," he said, fixing his gaze right between my eyes. "I was just going to correct the problem."

Though none of my small band of election frauders provided any of it, some good things may have happened in response to my demonic act of cleverness. The Queen Booth was considered one of the big moneymakers at the carnival, and the other classes had, of course, elected their most popular girls. The voting was particularly heavy that year. Remember, the entire population of the town was registered to vote, since the boxes were placed in virtually every retail outlet, and a visible running tally was kept daily. While members of the other classes stuffed the ballots to support their candidates, the town's adults took up Janice's cause in order to at least keep her in the running. When it was all over, the Queen Booth had made more money for its sponsoring class than during any other year. The universe must have a quirky sense of humor, because we were that class. I still feel fortunate that LeRoy Pain didn't think to make us donate our ill-gotten gains to the John Birch Society's war chest.

When the carnival itself wound down, all we freshman boys, most of whom normally would have headed home to watch "Friday Night Monsters" on TV, descended into the boys' locker room in the gym and donned sports jackets and ties (another avoid-Pain requirement), slicked down our hair, and returned for our requisite three dances.

Most of us sat in the darkness of the bleachers, discreetly flipping coins or playing rocks and scissors to see who would go next, then dutifully danced at arm's length, two jerky steps forward, one jerky step back, having to pass up the fast ones due to coordination deficit. I was the last to go in the first round. I took a deep breath, blew out hard, and approached. It wasn't the dance that bothered me; I'd taken square dancing and ballroom dancing from Mrs. Griffith since third grade, and she had always required every male student to dance with every female student at least once before we left our lessons. It was that I thought Janice knew. This shit had Chris Crutcher written all over it.

"May I have this dance?" I put out my hand. Janice smiled, reached out, and took it; Gene Gestrin looked relieved. It was turning out that the guy who brought her danced with her the least. We knew the rest of the school was watching; no other girls would dance with us until they'd seen each of us dance with Janice at least twice. The counterconspiracy was enormous. This was way less funny than I had imagined.

After a couple of false starts, Janice and I were in sync (which also hadn't been invented yet) and she placed her white-gloved hand on my shoulder. She probably looked better than on any day before or since. My aunt Nori, famous for making all the popular girls' prom dresses, had donated time and material to keep Janice from having to wear the dress her mother was married in. Some of the senior girls had helped with her makeup, and though she was still Janice Winthrop in our heads, there was the outline of what she might have been, had her life not been written all over her face.

"I know this was a joke . . . ," she said a few verses into the song.

"Naw, it wasn't a joke," I said. "We just thought you hadn't . . . "

"I know it was a joke . . . ," she said again, and I was hot and flushed from my failure as a liar. I knew once and for all why this wasn't funny.

" . . . but this is still the best night of my life."

I actually pulled her closer, just so I wouldn't have to look into her eyes. Later—much later—I would write a short story about an overweight kid with two sets of gay parents, who took nothing but shit from his peers, being voted Winter Ball king at his high school and coming away with a *moment* with the girl of his very bold dreams, a moment that would last a lifetime. I think I gave that story a happy ending out of wishful thinking; I'd be surprised if Janice's *moment* lasted a week. But at least she had the courage to turn it into one.

I look back over forty years. Janice dropped out of high school the next year and married a logger in his early forties. I think of that, knowing what I now know from walking arm in arm through private hells with people who have been savaged, and consider what her life must really have been like. I wonder about Janice's night as our carnival-queen candidate. The intent was insensitive and unkind, no question about that, but I have slim hopes about the effect of the result. I think of those lessons of relativity, how my father's coal furnace was freezing, and how warm, three-month-old Limburger cheese smells like roses under the right circumstances, and I trick myself into hoping that out of it all might have come a tiny oasis for a girl with the courage to find something special sifting through the rubble of my adolescent cruelty.

Conversations with Gawd

❖◆❖

8

MOST OF THE KIDS I KNEW GROWING UP, besides the Catholics and Mormons, attended the Red Brick Church because it had the best Sunday school; for all I know, the only one. You could get your kid Bible lessons and get him or her out of there before they got to the incomprehensible adult Bible lessons delivered later in church. It was a kind of come-one-come-all place with, I now see, a decided fundamentalist flair and about a fifty percent casualty rate on preachers who got involved with other people's wives or teenagers.

My parents weren't avid churchgoers, but they were more than willing to get rid of us for a couple of hours on any given Sunday, and my mother had a good enough alto voice to be a standout in the choir on special occasions. They always gave us a choice whether or not to attend, but for many of my early years I was consistent.

In fact, between my fifth and sixth year, my shiny face showed up exactly fifty-two times. I wanted the Prize; the mysterious, oft-alluded-to, never described reward for perfect attendance. It was very special, they said. You couldn't buy it in stores, they said. Be the first and only kid on your block to have one, they said. Only those who showed up *every* Sunday, for better or worse, in green-slime nose-running, projectile-vomiting queasiness and in health, would walk away with the mysterious, coveted Prize. Out of probably twenty-five or thirty kids, three of us made it. On Sunday of that fifty-second week, we stayed after Sunday school for grown-up church, to be celebrated and embraced for righteous tenacity before the entire congregation. The Reverend Pardee told the rapt parishioners that from among us might spring the next Billy Graham.

The perfect attendance award was laid in soft cotton inside a small, white, expensive-looking box. Inside, mounted on a brown plastic base, were thick greenish white plastic letters reading JESUS SAVES.

I had hoped for one of those little plastic frogmen you

could send away for from Kellogg's Frosted Flakes. You filled a little compartment on his foot with baking soda and when the baking soda soaked up water, he would actually *dive deep into your bathtub.*

JESUS SAVES.

My disappointment was brief. Reverend Pardee instructed the three of us to hold our trophies high for the rest of the congregation to see, then made the entire fifty-two weeks worth it. "These children, these lambs of God, will never be without this message," he said. "Spring or winter. Summer or fall." His intensity built. "Good times and bad. Sickness and health." We fidgeted now, swaying from foot to foot. And then he sprung the Good News, pointing at a church deacon to douse the lights. *"Day or night."* There was a slight gasp from the audience, and we looked up. JESUS SAVES, JESUS SAVES, JESUS SAVES was *glowing in the dark.*

I couldn't wait to get it home, flashing it briefly to my parents and brother on my lightning trip from the front door to the downstairs bedroom I shared with John. I pulled the curtains on the one small high window and turned out the lights.

The dim greenish glow of that same plastic they use to make glow-in-the-dark vampire teeth said it all: JESUS SAVES.

My brother came down to tell me Sunday breakfast was ready.

Sunday morning meant link sausage and waffles. My favorite.

I said I wasn't hungry.

"How come you're sitting in the dark?"

I nodded toward the shelf from which glowed the message of the lifeguard Jesus.

"You gonna sit here all day and look at that thing?"

"Yeah. You can come down if you want, too. We could put on our pajamas."

He picked it up to take a closer look and I yelled and jumped up, snatching it from his grasp and knocking it to the hardwood floor. I snatched it up. ESUS SAVES. The J glowed back at me from the floor.

Stunned, I stepped into my imaginary telephone booth, whipped off my imaginary glasses and suit jacket, and out stepped . . . bawlbaby. Fifty-two weeks of coloring the bearded, robed men and veiled women of Nazareth. Fifty-two weeks of memorizing the names of the disciples, never understanding whether or not they were the same guys as the apostles. Fifty-two weeks of singing "Jesus loves me, this I know . . . "

There was much wailing and gnashing of teeth. "I'm tellin'!" I convulsed. "You're really in trouble now."

"I didn't mean to break it," he said.

"You're s'posed to keep your hands off my stuff. You

never let me touch your stuff."

He looked around the room. "You can touch anything you want."

"No, sir. Too late."

He reached into his toy box. "Here," he said. "You can break some Tinkertoys."

Those Tinkertoys belonged to both of us. Plus, I was not about to even this up so easily. I had been wronged in a serious and spiritual way.

"No, sir, I'm not breakin' anything. I'm tellin'."

"I'm not the one who broke it," he said. "I just picked it up to look at it. You're the one who grabbed it out of my hand. What a stingy guts anyway. God probably had you break it because you're a stingy guts."

I shook my head hard. "Huh-uh. You're not s'posed to put your hands on my stuff."

"Stingy guts."

"I'm tellin'."

"Did you know Jesus had a big brother?"

"No, sir, Jesus did not have a big brother. And even if He did, I bet He made him keep his hands off His stuff."

"I'm not kidding. He had a big brother. That's where He got most of His big ideas. I even know what his name was."

Don't even try it, John. I'd been going to church for

fifty-two weeks straight, and there had been not one mention of Jesus' big brother.

"Nobody knows about him, at least not very many people. But he was actually smarter than Jesus. He wrote some of the stuff in the Bible for Him."

"Okay, if you're so smart, what was his name?"

"Not tellin'," he said. "You wouldn't believe me anyway." He picked up the Tinkertoys he had given me to break and put them back in the toy box.

Man, I had one short attention span. "I might believe you. What was his name?"

"You have to promise you'll believe me."

Even this early in life, this many years before I would be brutally gunned down with a Daisy Red Ryder BB gun, this should have had a familiar ring; but if this was true, I could take it back and be the smartest kid in my Sunday school class. "Okay," I said reluctantly. "Promise. I'll believe you. Tell me what was his name."

"Esus. And you're the only kid who has a glow-in-the-dark sign of him."

"Jesus had a big brother named Esus? He did not. You're a liar."

"You promised you'd believe me."

"That's no fair," I said. "There's nobody named Esus."

"Cross my heart," my brother said. "But he wasn't famous like Jesus, even though he was smarter. One of his eyes was poked out. That's why nobody talks about him. He wasn't famous."

"I'm still tellin'."

"I know," he said. "But if you do, they'll take your ESUS SAVES away from you because nobody's supposed to know about him. You're probably the only kid in the world who has a sign about him. Too bad you'll have to give it away."

"How come I have to give it away?"

"I told you, dummy, nobody knows about him. When you tell that I broke it, they're going to take it away. Nobody's supposed to know about Esus, even though he had most of the best ideas."

In order to maintain its glow, the plastic trinket needed to be held up to the light intermittently, so I plucked it off the shelf again and reached as high as I could toward the bulb burning in the middle of the ceiling. My brother, relieved that he may have just avoided the need to explain to my parents why he was touching my stuff, took it gingerly from me and held it the difference between our heights closer.

I don't know why I always felt the need to educate my friends when I learned some new bit of information most of the rest of the world didn't know, such as the secret existence of Jesus' older, smarter brother or, later, that you could crawl into our coal furnace and freeze or that the water coming out of our C tap was actually warm. But I did, and ended up on the wooden bench outside Mr. Mautz's Sunday school classroom the very next Sunday for what would become the first in a long string of blasphemous statements. John had his internal distant early warning system turned on high that morning, with which he intercepted me coming into the house, my lower lip quivering like an eggbeater, ready to tell my parents how I'd been wrongly banished from my Sunday school classroom. John reminded me that if I told them I got put out of the room I'd also have to tell them *why*, which would mark the last day of my special relationship with Esus.

That night before I got under the covers, I knelt next to my bed and prayed to Esus that Mautz would not remember to tell my parents about our Sunday school difficulties when he saw them on the street during the week. Esus answered my prayers.

My brother is a successful Seattle accountant now (hopefully not acquainted with any top-notch libel attorneys). It is rumored that a neon sign above his office reads ESUS SAVES . . . BY DOING BUSINESS WITH JOHN M. CRUTCHER, C.P.A. I haven't personally seen that sign.

Once I discovered the Red Brick Church would hold out on information as crucial as the existence of Jesus' older, smarter brother, I became skeptical of other information they were sending my way and, as I got older, found myself perched on the wooden bench outside my Sunday school classroom more times than a budding evangelist ought to, for demanding the answers to questions boys my age should not be asking. For instance, what kind of protective rain gear was Jonah wearing in the belly of that whale? The acid in my stomach, I had recently learned from my father, could and would dissolve a cherry seed. Certainly a big old fish like a whale put out a *lot* more acid than I did. Wouldn't whale stomach acid burn holes right through about anything a guy could get at a regular sporting-goods store? What material is tougher than a cherry seed?

To the bench.

Then there was the curious matter of a mark God put on Cain, Adam and Eve's kid, because he offed his brother. A mark that would last forever.

"What kind of a mark?" I wanted to know. "Was it like a birthmark or a tattoo or something?"

Mr. Robinson, my new Sunday school teacher, said it wasn't a birthmark or a tattoo, but it was permanent.

"Did they have mirrors in the olden days?" I asked.

"No, of course they didn't have mirrors," he said. "Mirrors were not invented yet, and besides Adam and Eve were not vain."

"So who cares?"

"What?"

"Whether Cain had a mark on him. You said Adam and Eve knew who did it, so they wouldn't need a mark to remind them, and that's all the people there were, right? I mean Adam and Eve were first, then Cain and Abel, then no Abel. There weren't any mirrors, so Cain wouldn't have to look at the mark, and there were no other people to see it. So who cares if he had one?"

Like Mautz before him, Robinson loved it when I asked a question he could put me in my too-smart-for-my-britches place answering. "The mark wasn't simply on Cain," he told me. "It was and is on all his descendants."

"You mean like his kids and grandkids and great-grand-kids and stuff?"

"That's right."

"So how come we can't see it today?"

"We can."

"Does anyone in this room have it?"

Robinson shook his head. "No, Chris, no one here has it."

"How do you know?"

"Because the mark was dark skin. Negroes are the descendants of Cain."

I didn't have my civil-rights sensibilities yet, but I was starting to get a bad feeling about God, one that had begun a short time earlier when I discovered He had *smote* a servant who touched the Ark of the Covenant to keep it from falling over and breaking. God had said not to touch it, but the guy was just trying to make sure it didn't get ruined, and God just up and smote him. *Now* I find out He not only punished Cain for killing his brother but all of Cain's descendants who weren't even thought of yet when Cain committed his felony, and now Robinson was telling me that's why they were slaves for a long time and still couldn't swim in public swimming pools or pee where white people peed or get good jobs.

"Does it really *say* that?" I asked. What Robinson didn't know was that, though I pretty much had to treat God like everyone else did in church, falling down on my knees and stuff to keep from being smote, I had a different contract with Him when I prayed at night in my bedroom, and He was a much friendlier guy. I had already told God I could talk longer if He would let me pray in bed instead of on my knees on the cold hardwood floor, and because of that comfort I'd spend a little more time telling Him about my day and getting familiar. God was a much less scary dude in my bedroom.

"Show me where it says that the mark was dark skin." I was up on my Bible stories, and I didn't remember anything like that.

"It doesn't actually say it," Robinson told me, "but it's known by religious scholars all over the world."

I said that wasn't fair, and Robinson said it wasn't my place to question God, and I said I wasn't questioning God, but it still wasn't fair.

To the bench.

I know it probably seemed as if I was always trying to prove my Sunday school teachers wrong, but what none of them understood was that I wanted them to be right. I wanted there to be some simple way life worked; a simple way God did His stuff. Though I certainly couldn't articulate it, I wanted life in general to be congruous with the way *my* life worked, which happened sometimes when I prayed at night and never happened in Sunday school. At the same time my religious mentors were telling me what a loving God the Christian God was, they were scaring the hell out of me telling me what He'd do if I didn't behave, things He'd *already* done to people back in biblical times.

My final Red Brick blowout occurred when I was in

junior high school, about a month before I bailed out for good and threw in with the Episcopalians because a certain second baseman who hadn't moved off base to stroke my hair when I was flat on my back next to home plate with my tooth in the bat, bleeding to death, started playing the piano for them.

It was time to fish or cut bait on getting baptized at the Red Brick Church. I'd been avoiding it for what seemed to me a very good reason. Get baptized and be cleansed of your sins. I wanted my money's worth, and the more sins I could get cleansed with one dip, the better I'd feel. Years before, my brother had been tricked into believing he wouldn't *want* to sin after being dunked, and came on a search-and-destroy mission early in the morning on the day of his baptism, intending to whack me around one more time before piety bound his hands. I spent more than three hours hiding in the rafters of the garage and in the fruit-and-preserves pantry in our basement listening for his footsteps. (That afternoon my mother and I accompanied him and the others to Arling Hot Springs for the baptism. Arling was a natural hot springs about seven miles out of town, situated between two large cattle ranches. The cows from both ranches grazed around the hot springs, and often in summertime you had to clear the cowpatties from the surface to get a good swim. When the Reverend Pardee had covered my brother's face with the holy cloth and immersed him, the vacuum created in the water sucked a perfect face-sized patty right over the spot where his head disappeared beneath the surface, and for one quick moment before Pardee cleared it away, I thought I got a vision of the true face of my brother. That remains, to this day, the best baptism I've ever witnessed.)

At any rate, I was still sneaking into my mother's purse on a daily basis to steal change for candy on the way to school, as well as snagging a couple of free candy bars each time I filled the candy machine at my dad's service station, and baptism was the safety net I had in place to clear me of my sins. I was also cussing like a banned-book writer most of the time and having no luck at my attempts to quit. I wanted all that under control before my baptism, and I didn't feel anywhere close. I already knew that the brain wasn't as easily rinsed off as the body, because it wasn't three hours after my brother's baptism that he'd been stalking me like the pre–Freddy Krueger prototype he was.

"That simply isn't Christian thinking," Reverend Hannaman said. Reverend Hannaman was the church's new preacher. "You're in junior high school now; most of your friends have already found Jesus. You simply don't manipulate the Lord so you can commit the optimum number of sins. You think He doesn't see what you're doing?"

"Even if He does," I said, "He has to go by the rules He made."

Hannaman was a tall, dark man, and though he wasn't imposing in the traditional sense, he had dark down. He looked even darker now. "Chris, this is not a game. This is life, and it is not to be blasphemed."

What I wish I'd known then, because I'd have said it, is this: "Oh, yes, it is, Mr. Hannaman. It's very much a game—and a good one—and the people who don't know the rules eat a lot of dark brown smelly stuff."

So, with the pressure on, I took the bull by the horns and ran for the Episcopalian church like the very devil was chasing me.

Reverend Tate put me directly into confirmation classes. He thought my observation of Jonah's protective gear was funny, and he assured me that dark skin was certainly not the mark of Cain. He was visibly angry at Mr. Robinson for saying so and warned me that people's interpretation of the Bible could be downright dangerous. I brought up several other questions that had come up over the years, such as what kind of God would pile the bad news up on a guy like Job just to see if he'd crack, or trick a guy like Abraham into thinking he had to make a human sacrifice of his own son just to see if he'd do it.

Reverend Tate stayed right with me. He said, "Chris, what was your all-time favorite children's book?"

I said *Horton Hatches the Egg*.

He said, "What was it about?"

I said it was about an elephant that took over hatching an egg for a lazy bird named Mayzie that didn't have the patience to sit there until the egg hatched.

"Was there a lesson?"

I said the lesson came at the bottom of almost every page. He meant what he said and said what he meant—and was one hundred percent faithful.

"And was Horton rewarded for his faithfulness?"

He was. The animal that came out of the egg was a tiny elephant with wings.

"Do you believe an elephant could hatch an egg?"

Of course I didn't.

"But the value is still in the story, right?"

I said, right.

"The important thing about the Bible is the message," Reverend Tate told me. "Some people believe every story is true; other people believe some and don't believe others. There are those who believe the entire book is meant to get a message across, that asking whether this thing or that thing really happened is of no consequence. It's just one of those things you'll have to decide."

He went on to tell me that finding my spirituality was a lifelong task, that there was no number of stories I was required to believe, that there was a difference between the Old Testament and the New Testament, but even so, it was my job to discover what I *really* believed. I could be confirmed and baptized in his church for simply making the attempt to discover that about myself. And nobody expected me to be perfect after my baptism. Life was a learning process, and we learned by making mistakes. The baptism didn't have to take place in a dung-filled hot springs, but rather right there in church, and I didn't have to really get wet. That Paula Whitson would be playing the piano that day sealed the deal.

Back in fifth grade, to kill time waiting for our parents to come set up our Christmas party, our teacher told us to write down all the words we could find from the letters in "Merry Christmas." The first word I saw was Chris and the second was Christ, and I put them down in that order. She was walking up one aisle and down the other, making sure we were on task. She stopped at my desk, pointed to my first two words, and told me to reverse their order. When I balked, she told the class I thought I was more important than Christ. I was embarrassed and humiliated for being "too big for my britches," and all in all it turned out to be a pretty shitty Christmas party. Forty-five years later I named a character in *Whale Talk* Chris just so I could retell that moment in fiction, because what I didn't consider then, but wholly believe now, was that Jesus would have been more than happy to let me put my name ahead of His, *particularly* if it would have made me feel big enough to fill my britches.

Anyone who reads my stories today knows I often throw a religious theme into the conflict; in a significant way in stories like *Staying Fat for Sarah Byrnes* and *Running Loose*, and through smart-ass side comments by characters in most of the others, so it is not surprising that students around the country often ask if I'm a Christian. I'm not, and it isn't because a few semiliterate mentors in my history were unable to explain Bible stories to me. Most of the reasons I won't go into here, but I will say it started when I realized the God who allowed me to get into my bed to converse with Him rather than kneel on the cold hardwood floor was a lot closer to the God in whose image I was supposed to be created than the one the Red Brick Church tried to use to frighten me into good behavior. The scientist in me refuses to let me believe that biology was altered for a brief moment a little over two thousand years ago to make way for a virgin birth. I think Jesus would have laughed at that notion (it wasn't His, by the way), so while I have no problem believing He was one wise and spiritually connected fellow and no problem capitalizing His pronoun, I don't subscribe to many of the stories and thoughts that have sprung up around Him.

As a child abuse and neglect therapist I do battle daily with Christians enamored of the Old Testament phrase "Spare the rod and spoil the child." No matter how far I stretch my imagination, it does not stretch far enough to include the image of a cool dude like Jesus taking a rod to a kid. I believe there was a big bang and that because of that we are all connected into infinity, and I know very little having to do with human beings that doesn't also have to do with connection. We want to be noticed, we want to be good enough, we want friends, and we want to be loved. We want our place to stand. I believe that spiritual men and women throughout history felt and feel these things at some core level, and the statement that we are created in the image of God is a *Duh!* because we are products of the universal flow of energy emanating from that bang. And that's a lot of bang for our buck. I say all that because when I answer no to the question "Are you a Christian?" there is always a certain sense of discomfort in the room, because it's nearly always a Christian who asks.

I look back to those nights in my bed, praying/talking with an intimate God who understood what I meant even when I couldn't articulate it; a God interested in my life and willing to let me have my dreams, willing to let me fail, patient enough to give me as many tries as it took to find a graceful way through all the scary stuff, a God eager and willing to forgive me when I couldn't find that grace.

Recently in an interview I was asked if I thought life is fair. Because the lives of many of my characters are so hard, the interviewer expected me to say that life is certainly and obviously not fair. But life is exactly fair. It has order and randomness and it moves through the universe without prejudice or passion. *People* aren't always fair, and it seems the less we know the more unfair we are, but I think that a big part of the business of religion should be to understand that *nothing* is fairer than life and that mysterious ways are mostly mysterious because of our ignorance.

A Different Kind of
Love Story

9

I MENTIONED BEFORE THAT PERTY GIRLS were my downfall, and at the onset of puberty, which didn't diminish that truth one bit, I focused in on Paula Whitson (good bat, great field) like a kid setting fire to an ant with a magnifying glass. I began finding things on the floor; pencils or pens, notebooks, money, and handing them to her saying I thought she had dropped them. She would let me know the article wasn't hers, smile politely, and say thanks anyway, probably wondering if she should run down to the county courthouse at lunchtime to swear out the early sixties version of a restraining order. On summer evenings her parents would take an after-dinner drive south toward Clear Creek Station and Smith's Ferry. To get to those exotic resort spots you had to pass the Crutchers' well-manicured lawn on your way out of town, and on each and every one of those evenings, between six-thirty and eight, on the off chance that Paula might be with them, I could be found on my front lawn, very close to Main Street, pretending to do push-ups and sit-ups in preparation for the upcoming football season, raking the lawn, brushing our dog, or performing some other activity you couldn't normally get me to do without a branding iron.

If for some reason her parents decided not to take that trip, I was held a prisoner of anticipation in my front yard until the sun settled atop West Mountain, growing goose bumps the size I wished for my biceps. The number of times a day a phantom crisis required me to rush past her house on some mission of mercy—on my feet in the early days and, after my fourteenth birthday, in my dad's '41 gray Chevy pickup—would make a lie of the laws of probability even if she had lived next door to an ER. That behavior today might well fall under stalker laws. Paula Whitson had plenty of chances to see me in action, but she must not have possessed the foresight to predict that my late-night talks with my mother about her continuing battle with alcohol had turned me into the go-to guy for dumping your troubles, because whatever there might have been about Paula Whitson that needed fixed, she wasn't bringing it to *this* Mr. Goodwrench.

About two months before the high-school White Christmas Ball during my sophomore year, my brother finally got tired of listening to me declaring my intentions and undying love for Paula, always followed by no action. A lot of guys wanted to take her out, he said while he held me on the couch in a headlock (and my sister ran around in circles yelling, "Lever has a girlfriend, Lever has a girlfriend"), but none of them would even be thinking about the White Christmas Ball yet. (Strategywise it was the romantic equivalent of fast breaking when your team is twenty points ahead with less than two minutes to go.) Why didn't I go in there and call her and get a date and then shut the hell up?

"I can't," I said. "What if she answered?"

"You would ask her to the dance," he said.

The very thought tangled my wiring.

"Go in there and call her," he said, "or I'm going to call her for you."

"Yeah, right. What would you say?"

"I'd say, 'Paula, this is John Crutcher. If you'll go to the White Christmas Ball with my brother, I'll put your first child through college."

"Funny. You're not going to call her."

He walked toward the phone.

My brother was not someone you wanted to dare. "Wait!" I said. "Okay, I'll do it. Just give me a minute."

He looked at his watch and started counting seconds.

The telephone was mounted on the wall just around the corner from the door leading to the basement. I stared at it. It looked unusable.

"You or me," my brother said. "Before we go to bed tonight, this is going to be done."

"Okay, tell you what. I'll dial all the numbers but the last one, then I'll stretch the cord around the corner into the basement stairway and close the door. When I yell, you dial the last number." It was the closest I could get to calling from under the covers.

My brother said, "Esus."

"Come on. It's the only way I can do this."

He shook his head. "Okay, you little dork. I'll do anything to get this over with."

I dialed the first numbers, then disappeared into the stairwell. I hyperventilated. I prayed. What if she said no? What if she said *yes*?

From the other side of the door, "Are you ready?"

Another deep breath.

"I'm dialing."

I heard the dialer whiz, kicked the door open, and slammed down the receiver. "*Man*, you gotta wait till I say 'Dial.'"

"Shit, I thought you fell asleep down there."

"I was just getting ready."

"Well, get ready quicker this time. I've got a home-work date."

We went through the ritual three more times until John dialed the last number and held the door shut. The first words Paula's dad heard when he picked up the handset were, "You son-of-a-bitch, lemme outta here!"

"Is that you, Chris Crutcher?"

"Uh, yeah. Uh, Mr. Whit— I mean, Les, is Paula there?"

"She has a cheerleaders' meeting at school. She'll be back about nine thirty. I'll tell her you called."

"Okay." I gritted my teeth. If she knows I called, she'll expect me to call back. "That would be great."

He hung up and I pushed on the door, but my brother was still leaning against it.

"Let me out. She isn't home."

"Liar."

I put the handset against the door and let him hear that her father had hung up, and he backed away.

We went through the entire procedure again from nine-thirty to about ten-fifteen. Paula answered the phone and said sure, she'd love to go with me, and was I calling from down in a well somewhere?

I said nope, just right here in the kitchen, then tried to find out what she'd be wearing because I wanted to get her a really nice corsage and I'd be there right on time as soon as we figured out what right on time was and she didn't have to worry about me honking because I'd come right to the door and she said, "Uh, it's two months away, we could talk about it at school."

I said okay, but in fact she would be very lucky (or unlucky, depending on your perspective) to see me at school for the next two months, because my mother would regale her mother with every detail of my suave phone manner on this night, and my brother would probably write an article for the school newspaper about what a hopeless dork his adopted brother was.

What happened next had to be the slow act of an angry God who punishes you for things you haven't even done yet, because unbeknownst to me there began growing, deep inside my brain stem, the Pimple That Would Be Stotan. This was not some molehill, or some prevolcanic rise, or even a small-to-medium Appalachian peak. This pimple would have its own spread in *National Geographic*. It was snow capped. It had climbing space for Sherpas.

And it reached its maximum height and breadth two days before the White Christmas Ball.

But I was lucky in those days to be intimately acquainted with one Ron Boyd, quarterback, point guard, and first-rate dermatologist who would later be the hand behind the power that made me spit my teeth out in front of Gerry Greene, who had a quick remedy for my leprous condition.

"Coke bottle treatment," he said.

"What do you want me to do, beat it to death?"

He looked more closely at the throbbing pustule. "You'd need something a lot bigger than a Coke bottle to kill that thing," he said. He rolled up his pant leg, pointing to a slight discoloration on his calf. "Big ol' ass boil on here just two days ago," he said, and he outlined the prescribed treatment.

That night as my parents lay sleeping, dreaming of their three children safe in their beds, I crept into the kitchen, quietly dropped a Coke bottle into a water-filled pan on the stove, and placed a wet washrag into the freezer. When the water came to a rolling boil and the rag was nearly stiff, I lifted the bottle out with tongs, wrapped it in the freezing washrag, and placed the mouth of the bottle over the mountainous zit, the idea being that as the air inside the bottle cooled and contracted, it would suck the core of the Vesuvian blemish, *whappo!*, into the bottle, rendering it harmless.

It did not come off as advertised.

As the air inside the bottle cooled and contracted, my forehead grew tighter and tighter. My eyes bulged. The pimple didn't pop, simply extended farther and farther into the bottleneck. *It wasn't working!* I pulled hard on the bottle to remove it, but it was sucking my face off my head. Man, I am going to the White Christmas Ball wearing a Coke bottle on my forehead! With that horrifying fate in mind, I gripped the bottle with both hands, gritted my teeth, and yanked. It popped free with the sound of two anteaters kissing in an echo chamber. Tremendous relief washed over me as I sank to the kitchen floor. Given the alternative, I was more than happy to escort the throbbing pustule to the Christmas dance. But later, when I gazed into the bathroom mirror, I changed my mind. The bottle had left a deep purple ring around the grossly offending blemish, forming a perfect three-dimensional bull's-eye right in the middle of my head.

Paula didn't say much when I showed up at her door in my brown blazer, slacks, white socks, and a stocking cap pulled low on my head, but later, as we moved across the dimly lit dance floor beneath fake cotton clouds and dangling paper snowflakes, two jerky steps forward, one jerky step back, at arm's length, she peered deeply into my eyes. "Nice of you to take off the hat," she said; then, looking closer, "Is that a corn plaster on your forehead?"

"Yeah," I said in my best John Wayne. "I was showing some of the freshman football players how to do a head spear in P.E. the other day and drove a loose rivet in the helmet I was using into my forehead. It's no big thing."

"That must have hurt," she said. "It got you right on that monstrous pimple."

It's hard to say whether it was the pimple or my primitive social graces (singing Christmas carols while gargling punch may have put her off), but when the Sadie Hawkins dance rolled around that next February, Paula Whitson treated herself to a date with a guy from her own class, both scholastically and maturationally. The fact that he was a *good-looking* guy, as well as a jock, may have had something to do with the fact that I went home and sailed my forty-five single of "Hey, Paula" by one-hit wonders Paul and Paula (a song, I believed up until I discovered she had gone elsewhere for companionship to the Sadie Hawkins dance, that was recorded with me in mind) into the vacant lot across the yard from my bedroom window.

My further actions in response to all that nearly got me thrown out of school and put off my chances of getting close to something soft and warm until after high-school graduation.

If the really popular girls couldn't see what a nice guy they were getting in me, or if they, in fact, *didn't want a nice guy*, which a number of astonishingly socially conscious pump jockeys who worked at my dad's service station were quick to tell me, maybe they liked being treated rough. At least that is the thinking that led me to place probably the most magnificent scab cultivated to that date in our hemisphere on Bonnie Heavrin's desk.

It was early spring of my sophomore year, only weeks after I had driven with a few select friends to the McCall Bowling Alley on the night of the Sadie Hawkins dance. (The selection of those friends was done by the girls of Cascade, Idaho, not asking them to the dance.) At any rate, basketball season was finished and preseason workouts for track had begun. Cascade is situated in a high mountain valley nearly a mile above sea level, so in a normal year there are still snowbanks piled higher than your little sister well into the spring, and the high-school track remains covered in white. Early track practices are held on the soggy, potholed back roads of town. That year Ron Nakatani, our high jumper, practiced his form wearing a rubber suit, bar-rolling into a snowbank.

At the end of the regular workout, Buzzy Estell and I were practicing baton exchanges for the second-string 400-yard relay. Okay, the third-string 400-yard relay. In those days the runner who was to receive the baton would extend his left arm straight to his side, fingers curled and touching the outer thigh. The runner passing the baton would slap it into the receiver's cupped fingers; the receiver would clutch it and run like hell.

On our first attempt Buzzy tried to slap the baton into my hand, stepped in a pothole, and missed, firing it onto the road directly in front of me, and I stepped on the baton at the same moment he stepped on the back of my track shoe. My right elbow was the first part of my body to hit the ground, and a huge strawberry, close to two-and-a-half inches in diameter, blossomed like the corsage I would have bought for Paula Whitson had she asked me to the Sadie Hawkins dance.

A week and a half later, I carefully peeled the gauze bandage off to reveal the beginnings of what would turn into a truly remarkable clot. The dark red base was marbled much as I believe Mars would look if yellow rivers fanned out over its surface. It stood a good quarter-inch high, and if I could re-create the exact mix of body fluids, I would sell it to the Hair Club, because what had been, before the accident, fine light peach fuzz had been fertilized into a bouquet of thick dark hairs that looked like rebars protruding from a broken concrete wall.

This was a truly awesome structure, and nurturing it must have been sucking needed blood and oxygen from my brain, because in that diminished state I convinced myself that if you could make a girl laugh or scream, she would be yours.

I protected the scab like a prematurely born puppy for nearly two months until, late one night, just before bedtime, I lifted one side, then the other, slowly, meticulously loosening it bit by bit all the way around until finally I removed it intact and undamaged. I dug through my storage closet to retrieve a small, expensive-looking box from a shelf of treasured mementos, removed my glow-in-the-dark ESUS SAVES, and laid the hairy scarab on the soft white cotton.

In the morning, after trying it out on Candy, to rave reviews, I hauled that baby to school, giddy in the face of an exciting, if romantically regressed, day.

Bonnie Heavrin was always late to first period. She was slender, with long blond hair and freckles, already a varsity cheerleader. Bonnie had been the first girl in our class to get boobs, had always dated older guys. She could sing country-western music like Patsy Cline, shrieked and grabbed on to you in scary movies, and had, for a very short time in her freshman year, run off to Florida with her boyfriend, who was about to be thrown in the county jail. After my undeniable rebuff at the Sadie Hawkins dance, I had decided Bonnie was my kind of girl.

As the bell rang, I removed the box from between the hard covers of my notebook, watching for Bonnie to make her late entrance. Five minutes later the door flew open, and as she made her customary apologies to the teacher, Mrs. Phelps, I removed the scab from the box like an artifact from the King Tut collection and placed it delicately atop her desktop. Mrs. Phelps accepted the apology as always and told Bonnie to sit down while class continued.

I stared at my book.

"What's this? What *is* this?" Out of the corner of my eye I watched as she gingerly touched it with a fingernail. "What is this? I've *seen* this. . . ." She glanced over at my elbow, bald and exposed for the first time in nearly two months, and screamed so high and shrill the hair on the back of the neck of every student in the classroom came to a stiff salute. She whisked the scab to the floor, jumped up, and tried to stomp it flat. I was on that floor in an instant, snatching at my treasure while dodging her heel, which sent it scooting across the newly waxed floor like a hairy red-and-yellow beetle. I snagged it and closed it quickly into the box at the same moment I noticed a second set of heels—three-inch stiletto heels, one toe tapping. One had to look no farther to know whose feet were stuffed into those. I stood up, staring at Mrs. Phelps's extended hand.

"It's a science project," I said.

"Give it to me."

"Okay, but I gotta have it back for science."

"Give it to me."

"It's a ladybug that was exposed to radiation," I said. "Be real careful with it."

Bonnie was hyperventilating. "It's that scab from his arm," she gasped. "He is *such* a pig."

"I was going to ask if you wanted to be my lab partner," I said to Bonnie. "This thing is an A for sure. I didn't know you'd get all queasy."

Bonnie shuddered. "It's a scab, Mrs. Phelps. Look at it. It was on his arm."

I already had an iffy relationship with Mrs. Phelps. Earlier in the year she had come into the classroom almost teary-eyed and announced that she had some very bad news. When someone in Cascade says they have some very bad news, particularly in that tone, you expect that someone has died, and it is most likely someone you know. We sat in silent anticipation.

"Robert Frost died yesterday," she said.

Before I could stop them, these words spilled out of my mouth: "Good, he can't write any more poems we have to read."

The people sitting in front of me in my row dropped their heads to their desks to avoid Mrs. Phelps's hand coming down the aisle aimed directly at my head, and she hit my ear so hard I had to put my palm on the floor to keep from being knocked out of my desk. It was a gesture my mother had long ago perfected, used by her, also, to silence my savage tongue.

That night my father raised his hand, palm out, just as we were beginning to eat. "I have some bad news," he said.

We looked up, waiting.

"Robert Frost died yesterday."

"Oh, man," I said. "Bummer."

Mrs. Phelps glared at me now, then at the pink spot on my elbow. "If I open this box and find that horrid scab, Chris Crutcher, I'm going to expel you from this English class. You'll get an F and have to take it over next year with the class behind you. If it is indeed a 'ladybug exposed to radiation,' take it to the science room, and I'll check with Mr. Payne at lunch. If, on the other hand, you say not one more word about it as a science project but rather take it down to the janitor's room and have Otto throw it into the furnace, we'll go on with this day as if this unfortunate event never happened."

Man. Two months in the making, and I was about to lose it after just one girl. I had a list. . . .

"What you do next is going to have a huge effect on your scholastic future," Mrs. Phelps said. "And you'd better do it quick."

I watched the fancy box burst into flames as Otto the janitor flipped it into the fiery furnace, a humbling end for the original container of the trinket that should have brought hope to the civilized world. ESUS SAVES.

Otto didn't check the contents of the box, however, so the scab rode home in my front pocket. For years, late at night in the dark of my bedroom, you could see it perched on the headboard of my bed, in the protective greenish glow of Esus, a ghoulish monument to the mystery of elusive romance.

Dead Boy Sledding, or Why Things Happen

10

I WONDER IF MR. DICKERSON would have beat out "The Star Spangled Banner" on Eddie Breidenbach's butt while we were killing time waiting for our parents to bring the cake and punch and popcorn balls to our second-grade Christmas party if he'd known Eddie would be dead before school started the next year.

Dickerson was the music teacher for the entire school, and he'd been making the rounds to the elementary classes all morning, playing a rhythm game. One student would pick a song and clap out the beat while the others guessed what it was. The person who guessed correctly got to clap the next song. It was fun, but Eddie started having a little too much fun, guessing the titles to "dirty songs" he'd learned from his older brothers.

Dickerson was a huge man, with dark curly hair and a voice famous for echoing "Figaro . . . Figaro, Figaro, Figaro, Figaro" off the walls of the school halls. He was a great guy unless you got him mad, which almost anyone could do at any time. Clara Hutchins was clapping, and Eddie called out "I Love To Go Swimmin' with Bare Nekked Women" as his guess, and Dickerson called him over. The look on Dickerson's face wiped the smiles off ours. Eddie stayed put. Dickerson called him over again. Eddie said no. Dickerson said now. Eddie said, "Make me." Dickerson did.

He bent Eddie over his knee, and Eddie tried to kick him, but Dickerson held his legs down with an elbow. Eddie's round face was flushed; the vein on his forehead stood out like a garden hose. "You better let me up," he said.

"Okay, kids," Dickerson said, "what's this one?" He began spanking out a song. We laughed and made some guesses, but Dickerson shook his head and spanked harder.

Eddie called Dickerson by his last name, minus the last five letters, and Dickerson's hands came down like drumsticks.

"I bet this is what you do to your fat wife," Eddie yelled, embarrassed now beyond caring, and Dickerson hammered harder.

"She's so fat I bet she doesn't even feel it!" Eddie screamed.

We no longer laughed, suddenly struck with the thought of our own seven-year-old butts stretched across Dickerson's knee. "'Oh, Say Can You See,'" Ron Nakatani yelled. "It's 'Oh, Say Can You See'!"

"Which verse?" Dickerson yelled, hammering so hard now that Eddie's teeth rattled.

Eddie came from a large Catholic family, with siblings of both sexes both older and younger than he. I played at their house sometimes. They were among the last in town to get indoor plumbing. Eddie's dad, Otto, was the school janitor, which was a cool thing because it meant Eddie could get you into places in the school that a lot of other kids never saw, like the boiler room and the tiny shop where Otto sometimes fixed things for kids in what little spare time he had.

Eddie didn't tell his dad what happened at the Christmas party because the prevailing parental philosophy of the day was "If you get in trouble at school, you're in twice as much trouble at home." Parents thought teachers were ordained. I remember after the party I told Eddie I bet he was pretty embarrassed. He said he was going to get even with Dickerson if it was the last thing he did. I told him I'd help him, because I wanted Eddie to be my friend so he could get me into the catacombs of the school, and I never liked "Figaro" anyway.

One day the following summer Eddie couldn't find anything to do. His buddies were all busy, and his sisters and their friends wanted to dress him up like a girl when he went to play with them. Otto was at the schoolhouse remodeling some small rooms just off the stage at the end of the gymnasium, so Eddie went up to hang out with him, maybe angry because there was no one to play with. Several sheets of Sheetrock were leaning against a wall in the gym, and Eddie must have kicked one of them, then turned and walked away. The piece he kicked had been standing nearly vertical, and it fell outward, caught him at the base of the neck, and snapped it. Eddie Breidenbach was dead at the age of seven. For a long time my untrained ear told me Eddie had been killed by sheep rock, and though I had *no* idea what that might look like or why sheep even needed it, I kept a close eye out for any.

When you're seven going on eight yourself, *dead* is a difficult concept to accommodate. Dead people were gone. They wouldn't be back. They were in Heaven, no matter where anyone said they would go while they were still alive, and they were walking around up there on streets paved with gold looking pretty much the same way they looked down here, only happier because God and Jesus and Esus were there. *We* should be happy for them, too. Only nobody ever seemed that happy. Several months earlier, when my granddad Glen had died, no one had seemed happy at all. I rounded the corner to our block on my way home from school to see cars parked bumper to bumper along the rock ledge next to the dirt road that ran alongside of our house. Inside, my grandmother sat on our couch sobbing. I had never even seen her cry. My mother took my arm as I stood in the doorway between the kitchen and living room and scooted me outside. She told me Glen had died, that I was to wait for my brother to come home and then stay outside and play with him. She had sent Candy to a baby-sitter.

I climbed up into the rafters of the garage and tried to decide what it meant. I would have some rugged bouts with death, some involving people I loved and some involving people I barely knew or didn't know at all. But this wasn't one of those bouts. This one merely set me to wishing and wondering. I wished I could go inside and make my grandmother feel better. She hadn't gone to the Red Brick Church enough to know that Glen was in a Better Place. A saint guy named Peter would meet him at the Pearly Gates, which I guessed were on the fence around Heaven. The streets inside the fence would have gold pavement, which I thought was good but wasn't totally sure because my granddad always had grease on his boots, but on the other hand, a couple of bricks off of that street would bring a guy about all the money he needed for the rest of his life according to my dad, who had once told me a solid gold brick would be worth enough to buy yourself a damn nice car with "a nice chunk of change" left over. I had the sense that Glen's greasy boots wouldn't get him into the same kind of trouble with God as they did with my grandmother. And since there was no disease in Heaven, he wouldn't have to eat milk toast all the time and have Sucaryl on his cereal because he had sugardi betees. But I didn't like the fact that it meant I would never see him again.

About a week after Eddie Breidenbach's funeral, I began having dreams about sledding with him. It was the middle of July, high eighties in the afternoons; but in the dream Summer's Hill was covered in three feet of snow, and we stood with other kids at the top with our red Flyer sleds. Eddie was without his sled and asked if we could ride double.

I said, "Sure. Hey, I thought you were dead."

"I am," he said.

"Where's your sled?"

"They don't got 'em in Heaven."

"Is that where you live?"

"Yup."

"What's it like?" I asked.

"You know. It's real nice and they got angels."

"Like with wings and stuff?"

Eddie nodded. "You gonna take me down the hill?"

"Sure, you want top or bottom?" Some kids sat on the sled when they rode double, bigger older person behind, guiding with his feet, while the smaller younger one sat between his legs. But I only felt safe lying on my stomach with the other guy riding on his stomach on top of me. It was hard to breathe, but you could guide the sled better with your hands, and since the hill dumped onto a road that wasn't blocked off for sledders, you wanted to be able to swerve into the ditch pretty quick to avoid getting a permanent residence with Eddie Breidenbach. Eddie and I had been about the same size.

"You take the bottom," he said. "I can't guide. I'm dead." When we got down the hill, he said, "That was fun. You can't go sledding in Heaven. They don't got snow."

I guessed it was pretty hard to sled on golden streets. We started back up the hill. "You ever see my granddad up there?"

"I don't think so."

"His real name's Glen Morris."

"Yeah, I know your granddad, but I never seen him."

I asked him to look real careful next time, and if he came back I'd let him ride double on the sled again, but before he could answer, my eyes blinked open to see the sky just over East Mountain turning pink and it was fifty degrees outside and the snow and Eddie melted away. As many times as I dreamed some variation of that dream, Eddie never guided the sled and he never remembered seeing my granddad.

When school resumed in the fall, Otto seemed exactly the same. He didn't talk much anyway, and he still fixed things around the school and fixed things for us kids down in his room. I started to tell him once about my dreams, but I was afraid I might make him sad, because even though people were supposed to be in a Better Place, most folks seemed to hurt at the emptiness.

It wasn't quite so bittersweet the next time I ran into the Reaper. I was eleven and had nearly perfected the art of throwing up at Little League games just before it was my turn to bat. Today, when someone uses the phrase "like a deer caught in the headlights," I automatically translate it into "like Chris Crutcher caught staring at a high inside beanball." The problem with playing Little League in Cascade, Idaho, was there weren't enough kids to play in age groups. Four teams, nine players on a team, ten if I was lucky, age range up to fourteen. Eleven-year-old Chris Crutcher wound up standing in the batter's box facing four-teen-year-old Jon Probst, later of slugfest fame, who had a fastball as nasty as his temper and zero control. When one of the bigger kids would get a hit off Jon, he'd get even by scaring the next younger kid into outer space. Very few of the younger, smaller kids could hit at all, so we were supposed to rely on our small strike zones to get on base so the big kids could knock us in. That required a good eye and the capacity for quick evasive action, an art I perfected by dropping to the good earth before the ball actually left Jon's hand—because once it had, and I saw it coming, I inevitably froze until the last second when I turned my back, took the hit between the shoulder blades, and squalled like the bawlbaby I had become.

"Shake it off and go to first," my coach would yell, embarrassed at my writhing in the dirt like a stomped-on garter snake. But I was a far-reaching thinker and knew if I were hurt badly enough, my stint as a target for the vengeful Jon Probst for that day was over. On one such day Coach disgustedly sent me home, but what seemed like a reprieve turned out to be the beginning of a nightmarish summer: C.C. vs. the Very Grim Reaper.

My parents stayed at the game, probably as disgusted as my coach by my less-than-manly behavior, and once I stumbled out of sight of the spectators, I dashed home to spend the last few innings in solitude, scouring the house for my dad's old *Playboys* and sneaking through my brother's storage closet to retrieve baseball cards I was sure he'd stolen from me. God, I loved solitude.

The newest issue of the *Saturday Evening Post* lay on the coffee table. I loved the *Saturday Evening Post*: the Norman Rockwell covers, the filler cartoons at the bottoms of many pages, sometimes even the articles. I always opened the magazine to the middle, about where I thought the cartoons began. On this day, there were no cartoons on that page, only the two-by-three picture of a six-year-old boy.

On the title page was a black-and-white picture of a vacant lot on the outskirts of Philadelphia. The article said a college student driving back from a weekend visit had noticed a refrigerator box in the lot, one he didn't remember seeing before. He stopped and found the body of a naked six-year-old boy, frozen in the winter temperatures. The caption under the boy said the picture was postmortem. I found the word in the dictionary. It meant the picture was taken after the boy was dead. Somebody cut this little boy's hair, the article said. Somebody bathed him and trimmed his nails. Does anyone out there know who he is? There were no faces on milk cartons back then, no "Have You Seen This Child?" ads in magazines and newspapers. I stared at the boy's face, the eyes unfocused, a small patch of skin peeling from his lower lip. They didn't know how long he'd been dead; his body wouldn't have decomposed in those temperatures. Back to the picture. Short blond hair, a cowlick in front; eyes a little slanted. Flat. Dead.

That evening I showed the picture to my brother. "I thought you were hurt," he said. "Shouldn't you be in the hospital or something?"

"Yeah, but look at this picture. I mean, do you know what postmortem is? They took this picture after this kid was dead."

"Yeah, I know what postmortem is. There should be a picture like that of you right now, after the way you were rolling in the dirt like you'd been shot. Man, why do you have to act like you're being crucified every time you get hurt a little?"

"Okay, I won't do that anymore. But look at this picture."

I showed it to my parents. My mom could tell how much it bothered me. My dad probably could, too, but he didn't like that it bothered me so much, so in his perception, it didn't.

I showed it to my sister and explained to her that the kid was dead. She said, "Oh, no, sir."

Sometime after midnight, I crept into John's room and

asked if I could sleep with him. He was groggy enough to let me in bed for about fifteen minutes, but then woke up enough to kick me out onto the floor. "Jeez, you little weirdo, go back to your room." No chance. I hadn't been in bed with my parents since I was five or six, but I crept downstairs to request asylum. That was my last decent night's sleep indoors that summer.

A stack of *Saturday Evening Post*s dating back to 1936 stood in our basement storage room. It wasn't a complete set—several issues from the war years were missing—but my mother collected as many as she could. It didn't take her long to discover I was stalking the Philadelphia kid, so instead of putting it with the rest, she hid it. Every day I'd find it. Every day she'd ask if I'd been looking at it, and every day I'd lie and say no, then she'd hide it somewhere else, and in the first hours of the following morning, when she'd gone to the service station to do some of my dad's light book-keeping, I'd ransack the house until I found it, then sit on the couch and stare at those eyes that were so obviously not staring back. I'd read the article again. I'd touch the picture. Then I'd put it back almost exactly as I'd found it, but not quite, because sometime in the evening my mom would accuse me of looking at it again. Why did I want to torture myself like that? she'd ask. Why not just let it go?

I found if I slept on the lawn in my sleeping bag, I was less afraid. If someone were really going to do me in, it would have been a lot easier to creep up on my sleeping bag in the middle of the lawn in the dead of night and ball peen me than to find a way into my second-story bedroom and dig through the 600 pounds of covers I was hidden beneath. But I'd go to bed and my room would start to feel like a closed refrigerator box, and I'd grab my sleeping bag and head for the great outdoors.

Then death began leaking all over everything. A picture of a twelve-year-old girl named Charlene Zahn showed up down at the post office. Charlene had disappeared from her Boise home, and the entire state was on the lookout for her. She and the Philadelphia boy began hanging out together in my dreams. Soon I was scouring the obituaries in the *Idaho Daily Statesman* with the zeal of a mail-order grief hustler. I knew the names of the people who died in Idaho on any given day better than I knew the TV schedule in the newspaper.

It may simply have been that time in my life when I realized that nothing was forever, that a person could be there one minute and not the next. I wasn't particularly worried about grieving survivors, though the thought of them made me sad; I wanted to know what it was like to be dead. And I started trying to be *very* good. I made daily attempts to stop swearing. I cut stealing money out of my mother's purse almost in half, cut ripping off the candy and pop machines at my dad's service station by almost forty percent. My daily prayer sessions could have landed me a guest spot on the Trinity Network, had it been invented yet. Lazarus became my new personal hero.

There is only one remedy for all that, though I didn't know it then. That remedy is time. At some point, a few months down the road, I simply said, If you're going to get me, Mr. Reaper, just do it. I'm tired of hiding under the covers until my sheets are soaked, tired of trying to discover whether every nocturnal sound is coming from the waking dead in my storage closet or the parade of zombies moving up Main Street in the dead of night to discover the phantom ladder leaning against the house outside my bedroom. Have at it. Hack me up. Suck my blood. Peel off my hide in two-inch strips. Kiss my ass. I'm going to sleep.

When I was a junior in high school, Alan Thompson's cousin mistook him for a deer and killed him. Alan was a relatively new kid; his family had moved down from McCall so his dad could take a job in the mill. He was pleasant, with a good sense of humor, not outstanding in any obvious way. He sat behind me in study hall, so we got to know each other in our mutual attempts to keep from doing homework.

I only knew Alan a few months before he was killed. I heard the news over the weekend, and it didn't faze me much; I've always had a delayed reaction to traumatic events. On the following Wednesday the majority of the high-school population migrated to the funeral over at the Mormon church, which was filled way over capacity because two busloads of students also came down from McCall. It was an open casket funeral, but I didn't look. I'd seen one dead kid too many. Later, as we stood outside the church watching the pallbearers, including Alan's cousin—the one who killed him—bring the casket to the hearse, his cousin's knees buckled and a moan escaped his throat that pierced my heart. I knew instinctively that, given the choice, I'd rather be Alan than his cousin. Death didn't haunt me like it did in the days of the Philadelphia boy, but the ache of loss set free by that boy's moan scooped out my insides. I went home that night praying the people I cared most about would stay alive until I could be a better human being, and asking a version of the same question I'd heard the pastor ask: "Why do bad things happen to good people?" which was, "Why does Alan Thompson get it when the Thornton brothers, who spend half their time threatening to kick my ass and the other half kicking it, roam the planet with impunity?" No good answer came, and I went through another period of trying to be good. Got the stealing down to about a third, though the swearing remained about the same. Shit.

I made it nearly through college holding death at arm's length—only old people died, people whose time had come—but when I was a senior, a close friend's girlfriend was killed in a senseless car accident.

Linc was one of the toughest guys I'd ever known; he still is. He was my age, but a year behind me in school. He'd had to take two shots at his senior year in high school because he punched out a student teacher for harassing his girlfriend. He was expelled for the rest of the year, and his father, every bit as tough as Linc, contacted a friend who was sailing around the world and bought Linc passage on the boat. To make a long story short, the boat shipwrecked and Linc had to pull several of the crew to shore. When he got back home, instead of receiving a hero's welcome from his father, his father enlisted him in the marine reserves, since he couldn't get back into school until the following year and the father didn't want Linc wasting his time. By the time I met Linc, he already owned his first bayonet.

You crossed Linc at your own peril. He had a "magic tooth," which I would years later insert, along with Linc himself, into my book *Stotan!* It was low-level magic. He'd had an abscessed front tooth before entering the marine reserves, and his dentist drilled a hole in the back to let the abscess drain. For some reason the hole was never filled in, and the swill that drained out of that tooth could easily bring a mink running with a smile on her face. If you disappointed Linc, or refused to do his bidding, he would clutch you by your shirtfront, bring you *very* close, suck the tooth, and blow in your face. If you survived, you honored his wishes. He was barrel chested and strong and redheaded and known for his creative capacity to get even. No one got a leg up on Linc. No one but the universe.

On New Year's Eve of my senior year in college, a bunch of the swimmers were together at a friend's house, watching bowl games, when our coach knocked. It was surreal seeing him there in the doorway; few of us had ever seen him away from the college or the pool. He called Linc into the kitchen. We glanced at one another, turned back to the game. When Linc came back, he said his girlfriend was dead.

For a while all the toughness ran out of my friend. He swam through workouts, hung out with us at our very edges, and complained to no one. Once in awhile he would come down the hall to my room in the wee hours of the morning and reminisce about the things he and his girlfriend had done together and the things he missed. Then he would walk back to his room, broken. Now I *really* wanted to know why bad things happen to good people. I demanded it.

After graduation I traveled with my college roommate and boyhood friend, Ron Nakatani, doing odd jobs, playing Route 66, and discovering my bachelor of arts degree plus a quarter was enough to get me a bad cup of coffee, so I scampered back to Eastern to get a teaching certificate, thinking that as much trouble as I had caused for teachers over the years, I could help teachers in general retaliate by causing the same amount of trouble for students. My student-teaching placement during the last quarter of that year took me to a high school in a small town outside Seattle where I would apprentice in English, psychology, sociology, and history.

About four weeks into my student-teaching term, a popular renegade point guard on the basketball team drowned while lake fishing in a boat when a quick, violent storm blew in. Charlie was a strong swimmer, but he had been fishing the lakeshore earlier in hip boots and had not bothered to take them off. A note posted on the teachers' bulletin board the next morning requested all teachers to report to the teacher's lounge before going to first period. There, the principal and counselors asked us to help the kids with their grief, help them understand. No one thought to help us understand. Most of the teachers walked out of the lounge like zombies, and the pall that fell over the school for the rest of the day was so thick you could almost taste it.

My master teacher was substituting for another teacher who had called in sick, and I was left alone with the class. I had no idea what to say. I didn't know Charlie well, but his edginess and quick smile were infectious, and I had only to think back to my college friend to imagine their loss. I told the kids to work on whatever they liked, or sit, or come up and talk. I placed a chair beside my desk and began grading papers and reading. Throughout the day several students sat in the chair and simply started talking. It scared me, so I didn't say much back, only nodded or shook my head in the appropriate places. Later many of them would say I had been a lot of help. It turned out to be my first clue to the nature of good therapy when I started working with people nearly ten years later: Shut the hell up; the person across from you is the expert on his or her feelings.

But this time death handed me a twist. At the end of the day another student, a heavy, uncoordinated freshman with thick glasses and bad teeth named Martin Korf (that's almost as appropriate as the name I gave Sarah Byrnes), walked across the school lawn headed for home, by himself as usual, bugging anyone within earshot with stupid songs and bad jokes. That was business as usual for Martin, but on this day it got him a number of mean, sometimes malicious, retorts. Martin looked confused and a little bit pleased; usually his weak attempts for attention didn't put a blip on anyone's radar, so today, of course, he got louder and stupider until someone knocked him down. He was still sitting on the ground yelling epithets at his assailant when the teacher I was with trotted over to help him up.

"That guy's a son of a bitchin' bastard," Martin said, brushing himself off.

"People are a little edgy today, Martin," the teacher said.

"Yeah? How come?"

"Well, because Charlie Post died."

"So?"

"A lot of people liked Charlie," the teacher said. "They'll miss him."

"I bet if I got drowned, everybody wouldn't get to sit around all day and not do work," Martin said. He picked up his books and walked off in his ungainly gait, and I realized that this day was not much different from any other day in the life of Martin Korf, other than that he could irritate people more easily. He was right. We wouldn't have suspended our regular schedules to let people grieve for him, because few people, teachers included, would have felt the need. It occurred to me that a lot of people in that school, allowed a secret ballot, would have voted Martin off the island long before Charlie.

The reverend in charge of Charlie's funeral asked God that same rhetorical question: Why do bad things happen to good people? and in keeping with the "Strange and Mysterious Ways" stance that was becoming all too familiar, he didn't give us an answer. I wondered if he'd have stated the question the same way had it been Martin Korf's funeral.

A student asked me recently why somebody always dies in my books. I said, because somebody is always dying in my life. As they say, without death there is no story. Probably a better way to say that is, without loss there is no story, and death is simply the trump card of loss.

At fifty-five, death is no longer a stranger to me. I have seen it heartless and I have seen it merciful. Because of my work in child abuse and neglect, I have seen, from up close and at a distance, babies and infants killed, survivors of drive-by shootings, attempted and realized suicides. Death lurks everywhere, every bit as much a part of life as birth.

In the spring of 1985, I was back in Cascade, Idaho,

visiting my parents. I'd brought the manuscript of *Stotan!* for them to read. At five o'clock on Easter morning, I felt a presence in the blackness of my room, flipped on the light to see my father standing in the doorway. For the first time *ever* in my life he said, "Buddy, I think I need your help." He was having a heart attack. I got him into the car and drove the few blocks to the hospital, where they stabilized him temporarily. We had a long talk that evening about what it felt like for him to believe it was probably over. He said it "scared me a little." He went to sleep, and I went back to my parents' house, talked with my mother until she fell asleep, and wondered what it might be like to be at that spot where you were forced to consider the value of your existence. It scared me a little.

The following morning I got up early to go see him, and as I approached the entrance, heard loud voices and scrambling in his room. I walked in to see two doctors pounding on his chest while a nurse ran for the electronics. I was situated just inside the doorway where I could see the action and also see the heart monitor placed outside the room. In the midst of the chaos, the man who was my father's chief political and personal rival in town coincidentally walked in to pick up a prescription. He looked over at the room, where everyone in town knew my father was, turned around with no expression, and walked out. Within minutes I watched the monitor flat line.

There and gone.

Later that day, after I had delivered the heartbreaking news to my mother and contacted relatives, I walked into my parents' bedroom and saw the manuscript of *Stotan!* lying on the headboard just above my father's side of the bed, open to the last page he had read. I gazed at the manuscript and thought how fortunate I was to have evidence of just exactly, to the page, how far my father knew me. I leafed through it, grateful for every word he'd read, anguished for every word he'd missed. I wondered if he'd liked it.

There and gone.

Because my brother, who is still fifty pounds heavier and infinitely stronger than I, would shoot me in the head with a BB gun right after he broke my collection of ESUS SAVES memorabilia, I won't tell you what I did with my father's ashes, but you can use your imagination. My dad was a bomber pilot, trained to identify his enemy, and to never give the enemy the last laugh. Like father, like son.

My mother lived another seven or eight years. Free now of the bonds of alcohol but not of the tight grip of nicotine, she developed early signs of emphysema. She stopped smoking the day they brought the oxygen machine and was able to stay several more years at home before losing so much lung capacity she chose to finish up at the extended care unit of Valley County Hospital, three blocks from the house in which she was born, rather than move in with one of her children. We traded off going down to visit, and I would make the 325-mile trip about once a month, understanding as I witnessed her desperate struggle to breathe that there truly are fates far worse than death. Toward the end of her life, coughing up a little bit of phlegm seemed Olympic. I remember the last time I visited, crawling up onto the hospital bed and holding her frail body, telling her it was all right to go between the sounds of her terrified wails. She couldn't die, and I wanted to know why bad things happen to good people. The bad thing in this instance was *not* dying.

I've seen death from many angles. Like I said, I'm fifty-five; I'll see it from more. I've seen it as an enemy and as a friend, as a curiosity. There is much more to learn, but it is clear that the best lessons about death come from the best lessons of life.

I know the answer to the question now, by the way: why bad things happen to good people and good things happen to bad people. It came from my inner editor, that part of me that forces the wordy writer in me to dump ninety percent of all modifiers: *Ask both questions again, minus the adjectives.*

"Why do things happen to people?"

Just because.

King of the Wild Frontier

11

IN THE SUMMER OF 1959 my father started letting me wait on customers by myself at the service station. Crutch believed in protocol, which means any employee who set foot on the pump island was in full Phillips 66 dress: clean, starched shirts with the Phillips 66 insignia above the left breast pocket; heavy, charcoal, pleated pants, cuffed at the bottom, with enough extra room in the butt and legs to shoplift a Volkswagen Beetle. That was *not* the style of the day. In fact we wore our jeans and cut-offs so tight you put them on with an airbrush gun. Not only could you count the change in our pockets from twenty-five feet, you could determine which coins were heads and which were tails. So it wasn't cool toolin' around as a Phillips 66 fashion plate, but as I said before, my dad was a World War II bomber pilot and he liked uniforms.

The uniform had utility, however. You had to be wearing it to catch the Mystery Motorist. As an incentive for employees in their service stations to be lookin' good and on their very best behavior, the Phillips Petroleum Company designated at random, each month, a number of its most loyal credit card customers as Mystery Motorists. If that Mystery Motorist were to receive Super Service from any pump jockey, the Motorist was to hand over, on the spot, a certificate redeemable for fifty dollars. Now, I started working there at age nine for twenty-five cents an hour (ten of which were earmarked for my savings account so I could put myself through college and not have to be limping out onto the pump island wearing that ridiculous getup trying to catch a Mystery Motorist when I was sixty). Though I received raises every year (up until I was a junior in college), I never made more than a buck and a quarter an hour. Given that, fifty bucks, translated into the currency of today, was equal to four million.

So in the summer of my twelfth year I pulled on that uniform daily, complete with Velcro no-buckle, no-scratch leather belt and very ugly ripple-soled shoes, and set out to catch me a Mystery Motorist.

One problem was that in a county as small as ours, the Mystery Motorist was likely someone you knew, someone like Bob Miles from Miles Construction, who did business with us exclusively. Proper Super Service included being at the driver's window as the car pulled to a stop. "Good morning/afternoon/evening, sir/ma'am. May I fill 'er up with Flite Fuel?" If they wanted a fill-up, you were to start the gas pumping, check the oil, water, battery level, and fan belt without being asked, wash front, back, and side windows, offer to check the tire pressure, and offer to vacuum out the car. You felt like Eddie Haskell in a baggy monkey suit.

So one morning around eight thirty Bob Miles drives up in the company pickup and I am standing by the driver's window as he rolls it down. "Good morning, sir. May I fill 'er up with Flite Fuel?"

Bob Miles says, "You've been jacking off."

My response would not earn me CIA Employee of the Month award. "I have not!" I yell. "No, sir! I haven't either! You can't prove it!"

Bob smiles and says, "Look at all those pimples. Fill 'er up with Flite Fuel. Hell, what am I saying? Make it regular."

I know he isn't the Mystery Motorist now, because

Mystery Motorists always let you fill 'er up with Flite Fuel, so I just want his damned pickup gassed and out of here so I can run into the restroom and survey in the mirror the damage from the fruits of my obsession with friction. Man, who knew *that* was the handle you used to pump out all these zits?

That night I prayed beside the bed on my hands and knees, fingers intertwined and locked in a dead man's grip. Without releasing that grip, I crawled under the covers with the resolve to reach some never-before-imagined level of celibacy, clear that the God of my fathers truly was the Old Testament God, one who would create such a gloriously spiritual-yet-forbidden feeling and then count on your face the number of times you achieved it. This had Ark of the Covenant written all over it. I brought to bear the willpower of my ancestors: Crutchers, Morrises, Pattersons, and Aherns alike. For almost ten minutes I clung to their legacy— before realizing eight out of ten of them couldn't resist the temptation of a third dessert. I untangled my fingers and said, "What the hell, what's one more pimple?"

So I figure if I'm going to spend my teenage years pockmarked, I'll turn it in my favor. What I need is that outdoorsy look. A rugged dude can accommodate a zit or two.

Enter Chuck Spence. Chuck Spence was the Valley County prosecutor who had spent eight years as a marine and would later return to active duty. Chuck Spence was a cross between Charlton Heston (the young, rugged, cowboy-Moses Charlton Heston) and Davy Crockett—a strong, handsome, physically fit man with a jawline you'd send away for. He was known to take a horse and a pack mule and disappear into the hills for days, fishing and hunting for food, totally comfortable in the wilderness. At about the same time I discovered my midnight (and midday and morning and afternoon) shenanigans were causing a *National Geographic* lesson on my face, Chuck was in the process of forming a Boy Scout troop. I would join the Boy Scouts and let Chuck toughen my body and my spirit to match my new ruddy complexion. There was an extra added attraction. Chuck's wife was Barbara Spence, a willowy dark beauty who taught dance and piano lessons. A year or so earlier I had signed up to take piano lessons after stumbling onto the information that she had an opening the half-hour before Paula Whitson's lesson every Wednesday after school. Suddenly I had discovered a deep yearning to become the next Liberace and begged my mother to sign me up.

Among Barbara Spence's piano prodigies, I was not. The maddeningly repetitive key stroking did not fit the temperament of a boy who had not, in his infancy, been allowed to launch his body onto the hardwood floor or bang his head against the bathtub at will, and my mother routinely ended my practice sessions within fifteen minutes of their onslaught when I began hammering the keys mercilessly with each mistake, breaking at least one commandment in the process. Each Wednesday afternoon, as I was finishing my lesson and Paula Whitson was showing up for hers, our conversations went like this:

PW: Weren't you working on that piece last week?

CC: I'm performing it at my recital.

PW: Weren't you working on it the week before, too?

CC: I don't remember, was I?

PW *(taking the music book from me):* Yeah, see? It says "Review" here. Five times.

CC: Yeah, it's a tough one. Bach, I think.

PW: Bach wrote "Row, Row, Row Your Boat"?

CC: Yeah, I think he called it something else back then. Oops, look, there's my mom. Gotta go.

The point is, not many upbeat Chris Crutcher stories were passing through the Spence household to Paula Whitson's ears, but I was about to change all that. I would join Boy

Scouts and turn my mind and body over to Chuck Spence and become the very embodiment of the craggy, ruddy-faced frontiersman, as well as the centerpiece of the Spences' evening dinner conversations. My imagination knew no bounds.

"Are you sure you want to do this?" my mother asked as I pulled on my coat to walk to the Legion Hall for my first meeting. "You didn't fare so well in Cub Scouts."

"That was just because I couldn't learn to tie that stupid necktie," I said. "Where we're going, people don't wear neckties."

"No," she said, "but they have to learn to tie knots. In ropes."

"And learn to tie knots in ropes I will," I said back. "Trust me, I was *made* for the outdoors."

"Are you sure they'll let you wear that coonskin cap?" she asked. "I think Boy Scouts have uniforms."

"They'll let me wear it," I said. "It's a coonskin cap, for crying out loud. Davy Crockett wore one. Daniel Boone. Those guys had to be the original Boy Scouts, if you think about it."

"Lose the coonskin cap, Crutcher," Chuck Spence said as I passed through the entrance to the Legion Hall. "This isn't play. We'll order uniforms tonight, and when they come each of you will be required to attend every meeting in full Boy Scout dress. Until then, slacks, collared shirts. Understood?"

Understood. Geez, this guy was a Stotan before there were Stotans. Besides, they couldn't be as ugly as my Phillips 66 uniforms. (My dad wouldn't let me wear the coonskin cap down there, either.)

I realized my Boy Scout career was following a familiar path the next summer at Camp Billy Rice, a summer scout camp near Warm Lake, about thirty miles into the hills over one-lane logging roads. Troop 235, made up of three patrols of eight scouts each and under the tutelage of former U.S. Marine Captain Charles Spence, showed up en masse for the last weeklong session of camp that year. Chuck had demanded that we be the most highly decorated troop of the entire summer. We would conduct ourselves as gentlemen at all times, spending twenty-four hours of each day being trustworthy, loyal, helpful, friendly, courteous, kind, obedient, cheerful, thrifty, brave, clean, and reverent, or we would walk—I mean, *march*—back home from Warm Lake. He mentioned something about Bataan. There's a reason I still don't like Charlton Heston.

It's too late to make a long story short, but suffice it to say that by the end of camp I had risen to my usual level of competence, just above those scouts whose parents had forced them into scoutdom to give themselves free Wednesday evenings. The final day was to be spent taking on challenges in archery, knot tying, rifle shooting, tracking, water sports, and safety, and proving once and for all that Chris Crutcher should have stayed with the piano. At each station the one or two scouts best at that particular activity would step up to take on the challenge. The full event was called the Gold Rush, and a patrol could earn up to eight gold nuggets at each station, depending on the competence of the participants.

Our patrol leader, Gary Hirai, was as competent as they come. It was his job to select which scouts would compete in which challenges. He was doing his best to match scouts with their strengths, and at each station he would look at me in a way I would learn later to recognize from coaches when they were deciding not to put me into a game. Look, consider, turn to another scout/athlete, fire a "maybe next time" glance, wink, and go on. Gary did that until there were no more next times. The last station was the rifle shoot, and all our other scouts had participated. We had earned more gold nuggets than any other patrol in the camp and had to earn only three more for our troop to win the summer. All I had to do was not screw up.

The rifle shoot station overlooked the lake. One staff member manned a clay pigeon launcher several feet away. The participant was handed a bolt-action .22-caliber rifle; he was to insert a bullet into the chamber, signal the staff member to launch the clay pigeon, then attempt to shoot it as it sailed over the lake. We were told that it is nearly impossible to hit a clay pigeon with a .22, that the exercise was about gun safety, really. I was relieved. I had proven on several occasions during the week at the rifle range that I couldn't hit the ground with a bullet, much less a moving target. But I knew gun safety from back in the days when my father wouldn't let John or me have a BB gun. This was in the bag. Gary stood behind me as the staff member set the launcher, calmly repeating those gun-safety rules. I listened and nodded, recognizing each one. This was akin to being given the last shot in a basketball game or being chosen as pinch hitter in the bottom of the ninth. And for once I was up to it.

The staff member charged with running the station, Marty Thorn (Fartin' Martin Thorn, the other staff members called him), handed me the rifle, then the bullet, and nodded. I pointed the barrel of the rifle at the sand, locked the shell into the chamber, nodded toward the launcher, and called, "Pull!" The clay pigeon shot out across the water like a nuclear Frisbee and I took aim, giving it lead, watching, squeezing the trigger. . . .

Click! The bullet didn't fire. I swung the barrel around until it leveled on that spot directly between Fartin' Martin Thorn's eyes and said, "What's the matter with this thing? It won't shoot."

The only thing faster than the speed with which that rifle was knocked out of my hands was the speed with which our patrol lost every one of our gold nuggets. They took nuggets away from us for *next* year. They took nuggets away from future patrols who might harbor later generations of Crutchers.

The craggy-faced Davy Crockett I longed to be was not to come out of Camp Billy Rice.

But according to Chuck Spence, every boy deserved at least one second chance. Toward the end of the summer he called to invite my brother and me to hike with him and the Bilbaos and Hirais up to Shirts Lake on West Mountain, looming behind our high valley town. It was a five-mile trek, straight up the mountain. We would be there a week, fish for our food, hike to the tallest peaks, find out what planet Earth was about at its most graceful. My mother said she was sure my brother would go but didn't know if I was up to it. Ha! No wonder people thought I was a momma's boy. My momma had no idea of the depths of my resolve to become a modern-day Jeremiah Johnson. I could scale West Mountain blindfolded with one arm tied to the opposite leg.

The Hirais and Bilbaos were *born* to take on this kind of challenge. They were natural athletes and outdoorsmen, could catch a rainbow trout in a mud puddle. From a DNA point of view my brother was probably a step down from them, but only a step, and he was tenacious and a fast learner.

I started walking daily. I filled my Boy Scout pack sack with cookies and candy bars and hiked the three blocks to work at the service station each day. I filled it with Coke and root beer and Orange Crush while at the station and walked the same distance back home. I ate and drank everything I carried to build my strength.

Turns out, three blocks twice a day toting a backpack filled with junk food does not Edmund Hillary make. This was the Fourth of July bike race all over again. A hundred yards into the hike I was fifty yards behind, and the only thing that burned more than my legs and lungs was my desire to go home. Hirais and Bilbaos sat on large rocks, patiently waiting for me to catch up. My brother was begging Chuck to keep some sense of respect for the Crutcher name and take me back. Chuck sternly but quietly ordered me to keep up, but these guys had actual muscles in their legs and were anxious to get to the top and start fishing. Maybe I should ride on the packhorse, I offered. The packhorse was at maximum capacity, Chuck said. Which thing would I like him to take off for me to ride? Seeing the expression on his face as I named the first three things, I realized that, like my parents, Chuck Spence sometimes asked questions to which he didn't want an answer.

After the third or fourth time I trailed back out of sight in the trees, Chuck ordered me to walk in front of everyone. Peer pressure. No one was allowed to pass me on the trail, but they were allowed to say anything in the way of encouragement, either positive or negative. They wanted to know if my feet hurt. They wanted to know if I could walk any slower. They wanted to know where I got the coonskin cap.

When we finally reached Shirts Lake (so named because, viewed from the peaks above, it resembled a shirttail), I wanted to eat and take a nap, and when I opened my pack to pop a couple of the twelve root beers I'd packed and crack open a package of chocolate-covered graham crackers, I was nearly beaten to death. Did I know how much twelve bottles of root beer weighed? And if I didn't know I wasn't supposed to bring them, why did I wrap them individually so they wouldn't clank together? Good questions, again no answer required.

The rainbow trout in Shirts Lake were known to jump out of the lake into your pockets. You could walk across Shirts Lake on the backs of rainbow trout, they were so plentiful. They were so crowded they'd gut themselves if you'd promise to take them out and eat them. A half hour into our first fishing session, the Bilbaos, the Hirais, and my brother all had their limits. I had zero fish. As crowded as they were, as overpopulated as was their homeland, not one was willing to suffer the humiliation of being caught by a whiny dweeb in a coonskin cap with root beer on his breath who couldn't get his hook in the water because it became hopelessly entangled in the bushes behind him. My temper caused me to jerk on the pole with all my might while loudly assailing the nature of Nature at the top of my lungs, leaving hook, line, and sinkers dangling from the bush. That same temper *forced* me to kick my creel into the water, losing all my extra equipment and bait.

The guys went back to camp to clean the fish and prepare the fire for lunch. Part of the frontier theme of this outing was to live off the land and water, so I stayed on the shore, casting the line Chuck Spence had disgustedly untangled for me. Still no fish ventured toward my hook.

Finally Chuck came back down to where I was fishing. "I'll be dogged," he said. "I've never seen *anyone* fish this lake as long as you have without even a bite. What are you using for bait?"

"Brrres," I mumbled.

"You should be using salmon eggs. Burrs?"

"Yeah, something like that."

"I've never heard of that. Reel 'er in. Let me see."

"It's okay. I think I just got a bite."

"Reel 'er in."

I reeled her in, bringing my bait into sight. Three green berries.

"What the hell are those?"

"Brrres," I mumbled again.

"Berries," he said. "Where did you get them?"

I pointed to a bush behind us. "Off that salmon-egg bush," I said.

Chuck Spence was a man of great patience. He and my father were friends. His wife and my mother were friends. We had all been known to have Thanksgiving dinners together. It would not have been advisable for him to do what his expression told me he wanted to do. "I'll make you a deal," he said, his voice pinched. "Lose the coonskin cap, and I'll catch your meals for you." He went on to suspend all frontiersman requisites for me, in order that the rest of our group could enjoy their camping trip.

That night a huge grizzly bear mauled me in my sleeping

bag. He lumbered right into the camp and picked me out like some kind of human candy bar. When he was finished, I was breathing through the sucking holes in my chest. I'd been huddled at the bottom of my bag, and initially when I felt his claws, I tried to scream, but no sounds would come out. No sound at all. At least in the dream. In reality, I screamed loud enough to send the packhorse fleeing back down the mountain.

I slept next to Chuck for the rest of the night, and the next day when he hiked back down the mountain to retrieve the horse, he took me with him and came back with only the horse. There would be no heroic *Field and Stream* stories passing through the Spence household to the ears of the fine pianist Paula Whitson, the coonskin cap was history, and my craggy face continued to be wasted on the body of a total wimp.

It turned out, as I discovered later, that Chuck Spence had been a soft kid himself, and he believed any kid could be hardened into a marine with patience and understanding. So just before Thanksgiving, he included me when he announced that the entire scout troop would be going on a winter overnight during the week between Christmas and New Year's. At the meeting he listed the winter gear required, then took us through the scout survival manual paragraph by paragraph. His most oft-uttered statement was, "Are you listening, Chris?"

Many bad decisions are made sitting in the privacy of one's bedroom with one's friends, allowing an imaginary world where dweebs rule to stand in for the real one. With the help of Jackie Craig and Spencer Hayes, who played Dewey and Louie to my Huey, I decided the Bilbaos and Hirais and John Crutchers of the world had nothing on me when it came to survival in the wild. In the face of all I knew about myself, in the face of the fact that we couldn't tie one square knot between us, in the face of the fact that we stood to actually freeze to death, we decided to be camp partners with *one another* and show nature and the rest of Troop 235 a thing or two.

"This isn't a good idea," Chuck said, telegraphing "Don't you remember West Mountain?" directly at me. "You guys should spread yourselves out with the more experienced campers."

"We've really been studying this survival book," I said, "and we're doing great in the rehearsals."

"The rehearsals have all been here in the Legion Hall," Chuck said. "It's sixty-eight degrees. There is no wind. There is no snow. There is no bitter cold."

"Yeah, but we're really getting it down."

Though I'm sure he didn't know the term, Chuck Spence liked karma. He was willing to let a lesson present itself and present itself and present itself until it was finally learned.

As I've stated, Cascade, Idaho, sits in a long valley in the Rocky Mountain range, nearly a mile above sea level. I have pictures of my six-foot, five-inch father standing atop the tank of his thousand-gallon gas delivery truck with one arm stretched as high as he can reach, and his fingers are still a good three feet below the top of the snowbank behind him. I used to walk the five blocks to school (oh-oh, here it comes . . .) in weather so cold you had to stop in three stores to steal candy—I mean, to keep from getting frostbite.

The Hirais and their cousin Ron Nakatani, who would lend his name to one of my favorite *Ironman* characters, formed one group. The Bilbaos and my brother and a couple of older kids formed another. Two other groups of kids who hunted and fished with their fathers in all weather over long weekends pooled their survival resources. Jackie Craig and Spencer Hayes and I needed no help from any of these dudes who thought they were so cool. I had a brand-new Boy Scout camp cook kit and a knife with scissors and saw blades and cutting edges and a leather punch and a fork and spoon. I had new boots. I had new mittens. All I lacked was a coonskin cap. I almost froze solid.

We parked the vans and walked maybe a half mile to the camping site. The temperature was above zero, and a light snow fell. The other campers immediately gathered wood and started fires, then built lean-tos to shelter themselves from the weather. They gathered more wood and put down tarps. Within an hour some of them were actually ice fishing.

Smokey the Bear had nothing to fear from Jackie and Spencer and me. We went through our six books of matches unable even to set fire to the newspapers we put under the wood we were too lazy to cut down to tinder and kindling. The lean-to structures built by the other groups might as well have been Egyptian pyramids for all the likelihood of our being able to construct one. An hour and a half into the experience, we were grousing at one another and shivering like wet puppies, unwilling to ask for help. We put one tarp down, our sleeping bags on top of that, another over the bags, crawled into the bags fully dressed at three o'clock in the afternoon, and went to bed.

Chuck Spence looked on in mild amusement. At dinnertime the Bilbaos and Hirais brought us cooked food, but we told them we'd already eaten.

The elements were kind for that time of year. The temperature never dipped below ten degrees, little wind blew, and only a skiff of snow fell. We awoke in the morning to a bright, crisp winter wonderland. Blue sky backed snow white trees in picture-postcard splendor. Gray smoke snaked skyward from four campfires, and the smell of sausage and pancakes wafted to us, shivering in the bottoms of our bags. Chuck Spence came by and shook us. Let's do it, guys. Get up and make a campfire. We're leaving in just a few hours. Let's have one success before you go home.

We counted to three about eight times before finally jumping up and cramming our feet into freezing boots, the only article of clothing that hadn't gone into the sleeping bags with us. Spencer got another book of matches from Chuck, and we agreed to follow the manual exactly and get a GODDAMN FIRE GOING this time. With numb fingers we chopped the kindling. A little moss from a nearby tree, then tinder, the kindling, some smaller sticks placed into a perfect tepee. I hadn't been this cold since my Christmas-tree-hunting expedition in grade school, but finally the fire crackled. Jackie dug sausages and bacon out of his pack, I pulled out the camp cook kit, and Spencer kept adding wood to the fire.

"You guys want to build that fire on more solid ground," Chuck said as he inspected our handiwork. "This snow has to be five feet deep; your fire will sink." He was right, it was already sinking, but we were freezing to death and none of us was about to go through the process of building another one. "And it's not the smartest thing to build your fire under a tree," he said. Jesus, Chuck, give us a break. It's the middle of winter, we could barely light our own tinder. We sure as hell weren't worried about catching a tree on fire. And even if we set the entire forest ablaze, *at least we'd be warm.*

The camp cook kit was rendered useless as the fire sank out of reach into the snow, and we began dropping sticks in to keep it going. Spencer got out his fishing pole, put a sausage on the hook, and dropped it down. The smell! The sizzling! Within moments the three of us stood over the heated hole, our fishing poles baited with sausages as if we were fishing for coyote pups. Get out your Polaroid, Chuck Spence. This should go into the manual under Boy Scout resourcefulness.

Spencer reeled in his first sausage; almost done . . . a few seconds more. He dropped it back. A slight rustling above us, a soft sliding sound, and the fire was *gone*! The heat of our fire had warmed the tree branches above us; the snow slid off and our fire disappeared as if by Mandrake the Magician. We stood with our fishing lines vanishing into the snow as if it were a lake, all traces of warmth or food a bitter illusion, looked at one another in horror, squinted our eyes, peeled back our lips, and transformed ourselves into a perfect trio of bawlbabies.

When Chuck Spence delivered me home that afternoon,

he asked my mother if she remembered how much she'd wanted her second child to be a girl. My mother said yes. Chuck Spence said, "He is."

My brother asked—no, begged—that I be given back to my biological parents.

On a warm, melting day about a week into April, the town doctor drove into my dad's service station. I was on the island before he could pull to a stop and gave him service so super he'd remember it today, were he living. He handed me his credit card and said, "I've been noticing you're having a little trouble with your complexion."

"I haven't touched it!" I yelled.

He smiled and opened his glove compartment, removing a paper bag filled with prescription soap and an ointment. "Wash with this three times a day," he said. "It won't get rid of them completely, but it will cut them down. And by the way, that's not how you get them. You're going into adolescence and your skin is oily and about all you can do is keep your face clean and it will pass."

"You mean . . . "

"And guess what," he said, handing me the certificate lying on his front seat. "You just caught yourself a Mystery Motorist."

A Requiem for Rosa Campbell

12

DINNERTIME IN THE CRUTCHER HOUSEHOLD was a finishing school for diners. My dad knew more rules for getting food around the table and into your mouth than there are cars on an L.A. freeway. "Kids," he was fond of saying, "eating is not a pretty thing. It's our job to make it as civilized an activity as possible." I remember being anxious about turning five, the age at which you were no longer allowed to eat green peas with a spoon. It would extend dinnertime by twenty maddening minutes.

After Glen died, my dad worked twelve to fifteen hours a day at the service station, or delivering gas and stove oil and diesel to smaller retailers and to farms and mining and logging operations around the county, so dinnertime was the only time of day we were all together. It always played to mixed reviews for me because, though I looked forward to seeing him, if you were in trouble, that's when it got talked about; and there were always the rules. He called them table manners, but to me they were rules.

My mother never sat at the table with us, but rather "pieced," as she called it, eating as she prepared the food at the counter or at the stove and drinking Tab and Jim Beam whiskey from a glass sitting in the closed cupboard behind my dad's head. At the height of her drinking she sipped away a full fifth, starting at four or so in the afternoon as she started cooking and stopping when her head hit the pillow around nine-thirty or ten, minutes before my dad would wake up from his after-dinner nap to watch the ten o'clock news followed by the Tonight Show with Johnny Carson.

So we're sitting at that small Formica table slid into a small nook in a very small kitchen. Big house, small kitchen. My mother hates that; she'd rather have it the other way around. Less space to clean, more to work. My dad sits at one end, my brother at the other, my sister, Candy, and I across from each other in the middle. My mother is nibbling on a piece of raw steak, which I will later come to call

Oklahoma sushi, from the stove between sips.

"Okay, that's it," Crutch says in response to someone asking for the potatoes, followed by no one picking up the potato bowl with the right hand, switching it to the left and passing cross-body to the right toward the person who made the request. "From now on when you want something on the table, say the name of the person closest to it. We don't need all the confusion." That's how a rule gets set in stone, in response to some phantom "need" only Crutch sees. So it has been said, *once*, so it shall be done. He will hold both passer and passee responsible for compliance: If someone asks for something and doesn't say the name of the person, no one is to pass it. The culinary version of Simon Says. It is the latest in a long list of edicts one starts learning at five, when he or she is, as I said, no longer allowed to eat peas with a spoon. (No wonder my mom doesn't like to sit down with us. It's tough enough to remember all these rules when you're *not* killing brain cells.)

Back to the business of eating and catching up with one another's days. My brother is in junior high school, and he's excited about a debate they're having at school tomorrow. Pro and con in the Old West: cattle ranchers versus sheepherders. John's saddling up with the cattle ranchers. I like that. Roy Rogers is a cowboy, and I don't know any shepherd heroes, with the possible exception of Jesus, and the sheep He moved from place to place were mostly His apostles. At this stage of my life, riding a golden palomino has it all over riding a cross. I imagine a stampeding herd of cattle. I imagine a stampeding herd of sheep. I imagine steak. I imagine *mutton*. No contest.

To keep my brother sharp, my dad gives him cattle, takes sheep, which delights John no end because he has *prepared* for this. My dad then proceeds to kick his ass, metaphorically, all over the kitchen. One animal has as much right as the other on the open range, which is, as advertised, open; and beyond that, one American has just as much right there as any other American. One by one, my dad shoots down my brother's arguments until John is nearly in tears and I'm about to turn in my six-guns for a shepherd's crook. "Elbows off the table," my dad says to Candy. "The table is for your food and your plate." To me: "Don't play with your food, Chris."

I tell him I'm not playing with it, I just can't keep the peas on the fork. I recite an old poem *he* taught me:

I EAT MY PEAS WITH HONEY,

I'VE DONE IT ALL MY LIFE.

IT MAKES THEM TASTE QUITE FUNNY,

BUT IT KEEPS THEM ON MY KNIFE.

He smiles. "Just don't play with your food."

My brother sits there gathering himself, probably wishing he had taken sheepherders for tomorrow's debate.

My dad says to him, "Okay, now you take the sheepherders."

John brightens. He has great short-term memory, prepares to take my dad down with his own arguments.

This is where I'm grateful for being the second child. I have long since learned to watch my brother navigate the faster rapids so I can see the best places to negotiate them when it's my turn. John goes with the basic human and animal rights Crutch just unloaded on him, and my dad hits him with the fact that the ranchers were there first and they have a right to the life they have carved out for themselves in that rugged country. The finer points pass over me, but one thing is clear. My brother had his butt kicked from the table to the sink; now it's getting kicked from the sink to the table. He is one pissed debater, drinking from his large glass of milk to keep from crying, then excusing himself from the table.

"Break your bread into quarters before you butter it," my dad says to me. "And you were right to take the butter from the butter plate with the butter knife, but you don't use it to butter your bread. Use your own knife. The butter knife is for everyone."

I'm almost ready to eat the bread dry. My dad watches John plop down in a chair in the living room, pissed and pouting. In a few minutes he'll join a cowboy gang so he can kick the sheepherders' butts tomorrow in school.

"So which one is right?" I ask my dad.

"Depends whether you're a sheepherder or a rancher," Crutch says.

"Yeah, but which one is *right*?"

"If you're going to play with those cookies," he tells me as I twist open an Oreo to lick out the frosting, "you're going to lose them."

I return the cookie to its original form. Not long ago I peeled all the chocolate frosting off a piece of cake to eat as a dessert for my dessert. I ate the cake, then excused myself for a minute to go to the bathroom and bleed off any hint of discomfort. Eating that frosting with no cake to cut the sweetness would be heaven. When I returned, the frosting was gone—into Crutch's stomach. "If you're going to play with your food," he told me, "you're going to lose it." And you can guess as to whether there was room for bawlbabies who had just lost their frosting at our dinner table.

I wait now for the answer to my question. "Neither," he says. "Both."

Obviously that can't be the real answer. Next he'll be

telling me to put my hands into freezing cold water or go hop into the furnace. Again. I tell him *one* of them had to be right.

He points to the corner of a candy-bar wrapper sticking out of my pocket. "What do you think that's worth?"

"You mean after I already ate part of it?"

"New."

"Five cents." (Boy, *those* were the days.)

"What if it were the only one left in the store?"

"It's still worth a nickel," I say. "It says so right on the wrapper."

"What if there were only one left in the store and Ron Boyd's right there with you and he wants it as badly as you do and he tells Woody he'll give him a dime?"

Damn. That Boyd . . .

"Okay," he says. "Let me make it easy. Say you're out in the desert. You've been there ten days without food, and you're almost ready to starve to death; I mean, drop over dead. You see an oasis in the distance but know you can't make it because you are so weak from hunger you can't take another step. You have ten thousand dollars in your pocket that you can spend on anything you want once you make it to safety, but you have no food and no water. *Now* Ron Boyd shows up with that candy bar. You offer him a nickel, and he says, 'No way, man. I'll give it to you for ten thousand dollars.' You say, 'That's all I've got,' and he says, 'Perfect. Give me the ten thousand, and I'll give you the candy bar.' What do you do?"

"Pay ten thousand dollars for a candy bar? No way."

"So you'd rather die. How much good is the ten thousand to you if you're dead?"

"What if I tried to give him *five* thousand?"

"Well, you're proving my point, but let's give it a try. I'll be Ron."

I'm into it. I get down on the desert sands of the kitchen floor. My mother steps over me to get another drink. I say, "Ron . . . Ron . . . I'll give you five thousand dollars for that candy bar."

My dad shakes his head emphatically. "Nope. Ten thousand or nothing. And you have fifteen seconds to decide because after that I'm going to eat it myself."

Aaaauuuuugh! "Wait! How about six thousand?"

"Ten seconds," my dad says. "Nine . . . eight . . . seven . . . "

"Okay! Okay! Ten thousand."

We pretend to make the exchange. My dad finds it necessary to remind me that under normal circumstances it is bad manners to lie down on the kitchen floor during dinner, but there was a lesson here, so on a one-time basis, it is permissible. The man has interesting priorities.

"There's not always a right answer," he says. "There's only an answer in *context*. Which is *right* about the candy bar? Is it worth five cents or ten thousand dollars?"

I point to my wrapper. "It says right here, five cents."

We are quiet a moment, and John has gathered himself and come back to the table. I say, "So you didn't answer my question. Who is right, the cowboys or the sheepherders?"

My dad's eyes roll: his most emphatic emotional expression. He says, "The goat men, Chris. The goat men."

He starts repairing the damage with my brother so John can go into school tomorrow and kick a little woolly ass, and as I excuse myself from the table—"May I be excused, please?" is the only proper avenue of escape—he turns to me. "You know that candy bar you have in your pocket?"

"Uh-huh."

"I'll buy you two of them if I don't get a note from Mr. Knee tomorrow telling me you got a bloody nose for trying to sell one for ten thousand dollars."

Candy spent the rest of the evening putting "Lever bought a candy bar for ten thousand dollars" to music.

I was seventeen when I knew I'd never be married. When I look back on that time, when all the vibrance of learning and interacting and relating was going on in the kitchen, my mother moved through it like a ghost waitress, refilling her glass, drinking herself inconspicuously into a state of numbness. Before I knew what she was doing, I thought she was solar powered. The sun went down and she got dumb. In fact, as the sun was setting, so were her brain cells. Sometimes I think part of the reason she drank was because my dad's kind of thinking scared her. She had so many unarticulated wounds of her own and wanted some way to address them simply, though she could certainly never give herself permission. She came from a time and a people who valued men's responses more than women's, so she seldom stood up for herself other than to get angry when she was totally fed up with not being heard. She was kind and helpful and sacrificial to a fault, and she seemed to feel inept as a mother and as a wife because she could never please except by staying out of the way and not challenging my father for fear of getting the cowboy/sheepherders treatment. So we went by the king's-in-his-castle rules, and the king had no respect for the expression of emotional pain. You could express it, just don't expect a response.

My parents were considered by the townspeople to have a solid marriage. There were few suspicions of infidelity and they never fought in public and seemed to respect each other.

My dad was an intelligent, relatively successful man who was always supported by his wife and whose kids were generally well behaved in public and would probably not grow up to go on welfare. They were community minded and accommodating, and you could always count on them to do their part, though my dad could be what the Bilbaos' mom described as "a little hard to get to know," which meant he was intimidating. It was a great package, but inside that package, for whatever reason, it fell to me to make my mother feel better. Because she could never please, she could never truly *be* pleased, but I'd work my ass off to do it anyway.

The evening scenario *around* that dinnertime interaction went something like this: Jewell would see Crutch coming up the walk out the kitchen window and pour him a gin and tonic, handing it to him as he came through the door. He drank it as he watched the evening news, rattled the ice when it was empty, which signaled her he was ready for his second. If for some reason the TV was louder than the ice clinking against the side of the glass and she didn't hear, he rattled it again and the second drink appeared. Then we had dinner, which Jewell swept through like a ghostly waitress, and afterward Crutch would have a glass of iced tea, stretch out on the couch to watch TV, and fall asleep, while my mother cleaned the kitchen and polished off the Jim Beam. I would sit in the living room, planning to go outside and play hide-and-go-seek or kick the can or ante-eye-over with my friends. Often I could hear them out there starting up the game, sometimes even calling my name to hurry and come out.

Now, understand that the front door to our house was a large double French door opening out onto a sprawling front lawn. The back door was a standard-sized door just off the kitchen that opened onto a patch of backyard. I could have escaped out the front without notice, simply hollering, "I'm going outside to play" as I disappeared through it. But that would have been unfair. The trick for me was to try to get through the kitchen past my grieving mother.

I'd walk through, pulling on my jacket. "I'm gonna go out and play for a while."

Sigh. "Okay, honey. Have a good time."

"What's wrong?"

"Oh, nothing. You just run along. I'll be fine."

"It sounds like there's something wrong."

"No, dear. I'm fine. You run along."

But I didn't. I'd stand and wait, feeling for a moment like a hit-and-run driver, wanting to go ahead, inching toward the door. . . .

"It's just hard, that's all."

Shit. "What's hard?"

And off it went. She was loosened up enough to lament about the sad state of world affairs or her life, which, at that degree of impairment, were one and the same. I did my best to convince her things weren't as bad as they felt (I learned that from watching her do it with her depressed friends), and she did her best not to be convinced, interrupting me every half hour or so to tell me to go outside or my friends would be done, and I'd say, "I'll go in a minute" and never do it. She'd finally go to bed and pass out; I'd go upstairs to my room with some faint feeling of having saved her. After "The Star-Spangled Banner" played to end the TV day, Crutch would go into the bedroom and read himself to sleep. My mother, by her own report, never had a hangover in her life, so she got up early in the morning, ahead of him, and fixed his breakfast. My father was a voracious reader— of any genre, fiction or nonfiction—and because he loved to read in a completely quiet house each morning, she went back to bed until it was time to get us up to go to school.

As I said, they seldom fought out loud and seemed to treat each other respectfully, at least as I understood respect at the time. They promoted and supported their kids' accomplishments, and no one in town knew the amounts of alcohol that were consumed in our house. *That's* what I thought marriage was, and I didn't want any part of it.

Though I could never have come to this conclusion *then*, I now look back at my parents' relationship without judgment. It wasn't a *good* thing that my dad could turn almost any situation into a PBS moment, any more than it was a *bad* thing that I felt responsible for my mother's emotional well-being, any more than it's good or bad that what I learned from all that probably shaped the best and worst parts of my relationships with women in the following years. I'm sure I shied away from traditional family life because of what I saw, but a traditional family life would surely have steered me in a different direction from the one I took, and I would likely not have had the experiences as a teacher and a therapist and a writer that I have had. It's easy to look back and say if things had been *perfect*, I could have accommodated all of those things into my life. But as a therapist I do not allow that word to be uttered in my office after the first session, because I believe the only reason for the existence of that word is to make us feel bad. It's the only word in the language (that I know of) that is defined in common usage by what *can't* be. It sets a vague standard that can't be met because it is never truly characterized. I prefer to think that we're all out here doing our best under the circumstances, looking at our world through the only eyes through which we can look at it: our own. The universe is kind enough to give us as many chances as we need to work through the things that cause us pain, and loving enough not to care whether or not we remedy them.

For the final seventeen years of my mother's life she was clean and sober, and discovered things about herself she might never have discovered had she not been impaired all those years and determined to stay free of that impairment. In the end, it is what it is.

I came back to work one more year in my father's service station during the summer after my freshman year in college and had an enlightening conversation with him. We were sitting in the front office during a lull in business, and I said, "So what was the big deal with all the table manners?"

"I just didn't want you to go out in the world and embarrass yourself."

I said, "Crutch, if I ask the guys I eat with to pass the bread, I better be ready to go long. If I take the butter from the butter plate with the butter knife, which is nonexistent, and put it on my plate before breaking my bread into quarters and buttering it a piece at a time, the butter melts on the hot plate, and all my buddies want to know if my condition has been diagnosed."

My father was unflappable. "I wasn't teaching you to eat with animals," he said. "It's for those times when you need them."

I said, "Something must have happened to you. This manners thing has to be the result of some trauma. I mean, I get your demand for Certified Clean Restrooms à la Phillips 66 and making us wear these nineteen-forties uniforms. But the manners—"

"Her name was Rosa Campbell," he said.

I made a mental note to remember that name.

"Her folks belonged to the Kellogg Country Club. Mine had just joined. I was a junior in high school, and her parents invited me and my parents to the club for dinner there because I'd been taking Rosa out and they wanted to get to know me. I had the etiquette thing down. My dad taught me everything I taught you. And then someone passed the bread. I took a piece from the plate and put it on my own. I broke it in half. I used the butter knife to get a patty of butter and placed it on the edge of my plate, replacing the butter knife on the butter plate. I broke one of the halves in half again, took a small piece of the butter with my own knife and began buttering my bread."

My god, how did the man ever get any food in him?

"And Rosa leaned over and whispered, 'Butter your

bread a little closer to the plate.'"

I said, "What?"

"Buddy, I've never been so embarrassed."

"Why didn't you reach across the table, take her soft neck gently in your hands, and pop her head off?"

"Because she was *right*."

"She may have been correct," I said, "but she sure wasn't right. Do you mean to tell me my dinners have been fraught with anxiety for eighteen years because some country club debutante called you out?"

"You had to be there."

My father is dead now; he died when he was sixty-two. He was twenty-four when I was born, so if Rosa is still alive, she's got to be around seventy-nine or eighty. She could easily still be living.

Rosa, if you're out there, be afraid. I'm coming for you.

———◆◆◆———

Becoming a Storyteller

◆▸◆◂◆

13

AN UNUSUAL PATH LEADS from my life as a coonskin-cap-wearing, pimply-faced, 123-pound offensive lineman with a string of spectacularly dismal attempts at romance to a storyteller of modest acclaim. Sometimes I stand before an auditorium filled with students or a banquet room filled with librarians and/or teachers, and I shake my head at the fact that I am living proof the universe will allow almost anything.

Due to our location in the center of a high valley surrounded by higher mountains, television came late to Cascade and was highly anticipated. Few homes had TV sets before my fifth-grade year. From what I had seen of TV on my infrequent trips to Boise, and in the homes of the few lucky townsfolk who got it ahead of the rest of us, I imagined a very different life: one in which I would lounge on the couch eating popcorn and drinking Coke, our living room having been transformed into a movie theater, staring into that magic box every possible moment. That imagination did not include time for homework. Our first TV set, of course, came with more rules than you might find at the Crutcher dinner table, compliments of one John W. Crutcher, aka Crutch. In the end, all the rules boiled down to one, and a river ran through it: TV time was earned with, and only with, matching homework time or homework completion. I got my first look at TV and was sold. I'd do my homework as fast as I could, slap it down on the table in front of my mom or dad, and turn the on knob. The more I watched, the more I loved it. By sixth grade I was the only kid in my class who could tell you the time and date of every program on both channels for any day of the week. I figured a guy ought to log about six or seven hours a day in front of that thing if he were going to be truly TV literate, and of course as I graduated from grade to grade and more homework was required, the matching mathematics was driving me crazy. Pretty soon I was trading a half hour for a half hour, having to make excruciating choices of which programs to watch and which to sacrifice, while also having to negotiate with the rest of my family members at any point of conflict. (If the conflict was with my father, it was resolved very quickly.) As I passed through junior high into high school, it became clearer and clearer that I needed to find some radical shortcut through my assignments.

My brother, John, was nearly three years older than I but preceded me in school by only two years, due to our birth months. John took his studies seriously and graduated as valedictorian of his class. On those few report-card days when he failed to get straight As, he pulled the drapes. I watched him through the insulation of those two years, the pressure he put on himself to succeed, the expectations from my parents that came with it, and decided I could use the fact that my mother had cured my temper by whacking my head against the bathtub to my advantage, claiming mild to moderate brain damage. From me, they could expect Cs. I came to imagine myself the perfect C student, to which there was a certain poetic balance, all my initials being C. C level was my perfect spot; my dad couldn't really get passionate about Cs in the way he could get passionate about Ds and downright righteous about Fs. For Cs he was only irritated, a state in which I kind of liked to keep him. A guy shouldn't make things too easy for an ex-bomber pilot.

I could earn Cs with a minimum of time and effort directed at schoolwork, but what I really wanted was to earn them with no effort, and that quest may actually have bumped me in the direction of future storyteller: I'm headed for the storage closet off John's bedroom one afternoon in my freshman year, to root around for old baseball cards he tricked me out of through the years. ("Man, I guess I'm doing this because you're my brother," he'd say, "and I must be out of my mind, but I'll give you *three* Marv Throneberrys and two Joe Garagiolas for this one bent Mickey Mantle and a Hank Aaron.") I enter this closet on penalty of death if he catches me, because this closet is the inner sanctum of his inner sanctum, ground where even Moses would remove his shoes. But I am safe, because John's off with Bonnie Heavrin—soon to be traumatized by a glorious hairy scab—and I know by the whisker burns I've noticed on her chin lately that he will not be back soon.

The closet is a huge walk-in with unfinished walls and a single bulb dangling on a frayed cord from the ceiling just above the entrance. The switch is broken, so you simply screw the bulb tight. I open the door, reach up, and twist the bulb, and immediately hear celestial music . . . because in the back of my brother's closet is every assignment he's ever done. They are separated by year and by class: his freshman year on the left, his sophomore year next to it, what has been completed to date of his junior year . . . *my* freshman year, *my* sophomore year, *my* junior year. I instantly become what I now believe is one of the first recorded academic ecologists, because for the rest of my high-school career I will recycle every bit of that at which I now stare in awed and thankful reverence.

I'll have to do a *little* work, because I don't want to be stuck with As and the expectations that go with them, so I'll misspell some words, come to some wrong conclusions, miss some math answers by a decimal point or a few digits, hand those babies in, and migrate toward TV Land.

By the middle of my sophomore year I have my homework time down to about a half hour a day, counting the fifteen minutes I take getting in and out of the magic closet undetected, taking pains to replace each paper or project exactly as I found it. This is far too valuable a resource to be handled in my usual shoddy manner. I am lulling myself into near illiteracy. But there are a few holes in my system, and I sometimes trace my writing career back to one of those forty-below winter days of that same year.

When we get that kind of nostril-freezing weather, everyone gets to school early because it's the warmest building in town, and I enter my sophomore English classroom about forty minutes early, noticing a number of finished projects on my fellow students' desks as I move through the rows to my desk.

I drop my books and elbow Larry Logue. "What's that?" I ask, pointing to his paper.

"Book report," he says.

"What book report?"

"The book report that's due at the start of the period," he says.

Shit. Cascade is small, but it's not small enough for me to run home and get one of my brother's reports, copy it over, and get it back in time to hand it in as the bell rings. But I never work without a net. The before-school librarian is Nancy Roberts, a girl in my class, and I just happen to know, because it is the kind of information a man of my limited integrity *needs* to know, that behind the librarian's desk in a locked room is a set of books called Master Plots, which contains a synopsis of each of a great number of classics. The operative word here is "synopsis."

I have been working at my father's service station since I was nine years old. I have money. I'm down to the library and on my knees before the checkout desk in the time it takes to say "*A Tale of Two Cities*," begging Nancy Roberts for time in that room at a buck a minute, but Nancy has a better memory for my past gross inappropriateness with her than I would have counted on and sends me packing. Never leave your destiny in the hands of a girl who holds a grudge.

I'm approaching panic mode. While Cs may be borderline tolerable in my household, showing up with no homework is a mortal sin, and I am setting records that would make my track coach proud, dashing back to the classroom to offer a king's ransom for even an old junior high report. No reports come forward, and interest mounts. Maybe Crutcher will finally pay for his astonishing lethargy.

Then it occurs to me: Mrs. Phelps, my English teacher, might be smart and well read, but no way has she read every book ever written. I can make this baby up. I scribble a title onto the center of the top line of my three-ring binder, and a story begins forming through the panic signals in my brain. It's a brilliant story, really—for about three sentences, at which time it starts to get stupid, and does not stop getting stupid until it reaches Ripley's Believe It or Not! status. But I'm not worried about that because when I get to the critique, I'll just say, "This is the stupidest story I've ever read. I don't see how it even got published."

So I write an idiotic report followed by a critique worthy of a disgruntled postman critiquing his delivery manual, read it over quickly. Aaaugh! No author! And I'm in full panic mode now, a condition that allows me to recall the names of only two authors: Mark Twain and Ernest Hemingway. Mrs. Phelps may not have read every book ever written, but she'll know in a heartbeat that neither Mark nor Ernie wrote this piece of shit, so I'm out of my desk and down to the office, where the Boise Yellow Pages lies mercifully open on the secretary's desk. I take out my pen, close my eyes, and drop it point first onto some plumber, who becomes the author of my first novel.

Now that's not a paper you put on top of the pile. You slide it into the middle, where you figure she'll be about two hours into her grading, head bobbing, maybe a little drool on the page, give me my C and get on with it. At the sound of the bell I slide it in there. But as I'm walking back toward my desk the thing happens that happens to all who would seek and take the low road: The paranoids grab me by the throat. Man, I am in *so* much trouble.

By the end of the following period I figure Mrs. Phelps has already looked through the reports and probably knows, by lunch I figure she's called my dad, and by midafternoon I'm expecting the county sheriff. Luckily the sheriff is my uncle, so at least I won't go out in cuffs.

But then it occurs to me what my father would say if she

really called him: "Let's give him a chance to tell on himself," because my dad is one of those guys who *always* says, "Chris, it would have gone a lot easier on you if you'd just told the truth." But if you do tell the truth, you don't know what would have happened if you didn't, so even with all the mental illness ricocheting around the inside of my skull, I decide to wait.

Correcting those reports is a three-day project for Mrs. Phelps, and by the day they are to be returned, I've lost about fifteen pounds in nervous runoff. Cascade School is one of those old two-story buildings with solid hardwood floors, and as Mrs. Phelps, in her three-inch-high heels, comes down the hall, it is dead man walkin'. I put my head in my arms and openly defy the new law prohibiting prayer in schools. Mrs. Phelps enters, followed quickly by the sound of the reports slapping onto the surface of each person's desk. I'm fully expecting to feel the lobe of my ear between her thumb and forefinger as she drags me to the front of the classroom to make a public display of the banishment of a worthless no-account scum cheater. At this point, I'd be satisfied with an F. I just don't want to be caught.

My paper slaps onto the surface of my desk beside my head, and I whip through the twenty-third psalm, cross myself, promise to keep my hands out of my pajama bottoms for six months if this turns out in my favor, and sneak a look: A minus. The minus is circled, and beside it Mrs. Phelps left me a note. *This was an excellent report; I especially enjoyed the critique. I docked you half a grade because you didn't clear the book with me before you read it.* I stare. I read it again. I thank the Lord and silently tell Him I only meant six *days*—five days longer than my previous record.

I usually tell that story to an audience of at least ninety percent students, drastically increasing my chances of a favorable response. (The other ten percent can be heard whispering—loudly and rudely—"Are we *paying* this guy?") But the rest of the story is that I was thirty-five when I began writing because I had to catch up on all those stories I missed. Simple fact: If I don't read, I don't write. Serendipity *did* get me to read one book during my high-school years. Mrs. Phelps assigned us *To Kill a Mockingbird* in the latter part of my sophomore year. My brother didn't have a *Mockingbird* report stashed in his storage closet of infinite goodies because it was a best-seller, only recently out in paperback. I read the front and back covers, hoping to glean enough information to sketch out a C-minus report, but when that wasn't sufficient, I began reading the first chapter and simply couldn't put it down. (When I say I couldn't put a book down, I mean I read it inside a month.) I couldn't believe this was a book. It didn't even give me a headache. I wanted to know Scout and Jem and Dill. I wanted to sit on the Finchs' porch on a warm summer evening and listen to Atticus's wisdom, watch him draw a bead on that rabid dog, and feel bad that he had to pull the trigger.

Mrs. Phelps probably didn't know it, but she had me. All she had to do was give me another book like that, but instead she gave me *Silas Marner*. I have often said the only thing worse than *being* Silas Marner is having to read about him, and I remain unbowed in that opinion. My worst fears were realized. Only one good book had been written. And now I'd already read it.

In my junior year in college I had the good fortune of becoming friends with Terry Davis, future author of *Vision Quest, Mysterious Ways*, and *If Rock and Roll Were a Machine*. Coincidence brought us together again several years after graduation (he graduated on the dean's list; I graduated magna cum lucky) in the San Francisco Bay area, where he attended Stanford University on a Wallace Stegner Fellowship, and I taught in, then directed, an alternative school in Oakland for students who weren't making it in the Oakland public schools. Davis and I would meet every

Friday, go for a run, have dinner and a couple of beers while he read chapters from his first draft of *Vision Quest*. As I've said, I was never much of a student, but this was a look at storytelling from the inside, which is how I learn best. He would read a chapter, we would talk about what worked and what didn't, share responses to the characters. Then Terry would take it home and work it over and bring it back, always better, always deeper.

I was amazed at his process, but when we were finished, I realized he hadn't done anything I couldn't do, if I started with a good story and the willingness to hang in there long enough to tell it. That brush with the true guts of story-telling gave me the courage to try my hand at it. So I read many more books of fiction, kept my consciousness focused on that hot spot in me that came up with my first faked book report, and ventured out.

By the time I finished *Running Loose*, Terry had moved back to the Northwest and I was finishing up in the bay area, so I sent him a copy of the manuscript for a critique. Now Terry is nothing if not polite, and would never have told me I should not have wasted my money on the paper I printed it on (particularly since he knew I was not above undercutting him on the way to the hoop in a game of one-on-one, sending him crashing to the concrete headfirst, thereby rendering him incapable of producing a second novel, but he called me at two o'clock in the morning to say he loved it, so I knew I had at least kept him up. He said he would call Liz Darhansoff, his agent, and tell her it was coming, and that I should get the manuscript in the mail as quickly as possible. As quickly as possible was however long it took me to pull on a long T-shirt over my undershorts and ride my motorcycle into Berkeley, where I dropped the envelope through the slot and was immediately swept over with the exact same feeling I'd had when I slid that bogus report into the middle of Mrs. Phelps's pile . . . times sixty.

The next day I went back over my copy and found missed periods. I found typos. I found gross stupidity. I found a monstrous piece of shit . . . which turned into a masterpiece the following Friday morning when I picked up the phone.

"Is Chris Crutcher there?"

"This is Chris."

"This is Liz Darhansoff."

She can't just drop me a postcard saying it's a piece of shit, she has to call.

"Chris?"

"Yes."

"I've just finished your manuscript"—*and we're having it*

rolled professionally by the Charmin people to sell as toilet paper all over New York City; we've changed the title to simply Running—"and I loved it. I'd like to represent it."

Silence.

"Chris?"

"Yes."

"Did you hear me?"

"Who is this, really?"

"It's Liz Darhansoff. Did you hear me?"

"Yes, I heard you. What did you say?"

"I said I'd like to represent your book."

Who knows how many conversations I had with Liz after that before she allowed herself to believe she wasn't representing some total hick Cascade Rambler oyster-chucking coonskin-capped idiot. Many, I'm sure. Bless her heart, she didn't send me any rejection slips until she had sold the book to Susan Hirschman at Greenwillow Books. Susan most certainly had done therapy on a number of first-time authors, because she was able to deftly shut me up before I launched into my third hour of babble about how she would never be sorry because I would make her proud and never miss a deadline on any of the great books I had yet to write.

Let me say this about getting published. The day the padded envelope from Greenwillow Books, containing the first copy of your first book, appears in your mailbox, you're almost afraid to open it and burst the bubble, but when you do, it's about three times as good as catching a Mystery Motorist and discovering zits aren't caused by hormonal indiscretion on the same day.

Though I had read many books of fiction by the time I finally put pen to paper, I had no idea about genre, and certainly no idea about the rules of the genre into which I was entering. That's good, because rules get into my head like table manners and make me spill my milk thinking about them, so I tend to let them ride.

At the time I began writing *Running Loose*, I had very recently spent ten years with kids from the streets of Oakland. Apart from that, I grew up in a lumber town where you found your weekend entertainment going downtown to see if some logger was going to get oiled up in the Chief or the Valley Club and try to kick some cowboy's butt, so harsh language came rather naturally. When Susan Hirschman began working on the manuscript with me, she told me Greenwillow was willing to publish my story in whatever form I chose, but I had used a certain two words in such excess that it might affect sales, given that librarians and teachers would be the first people to make the decision to buy it or not.

In its original form *Running Loose* was a three-hundred-page epic. I removed two words and it became a two-hundred-page coming-of-age novel. During that editing time, when one of my mother's friends asked her how I was doing, my mom told her she hadn't heard from me for two weeks, that she thought I was holed up at my typewriter unfucking my book.

Even with that, *Running Loose* brought me to the place where I would have to consider what I would write about and what language I would write it in.

When I was in fourth grade I overheard a high-school kid named Alan Donovan, who worked for my dad, telling a bunch of his buddies who were at the station working on their cars that he had taken Alicia Franklin to the movie down in Boise, and while she went to the restroom, he ripped a hole in the bottom of his popcorn bag and put his "thing" up through it. "At first she was surprised, and then really pissed," he said, "but when she got a sense of the pure heft of it, well, she got excited and wouldn't let go." At nine years old I had no idea what was supposed to have happened inside that popcorn bag, but I spent several anxious hours in the principal's office after my teacher discovered why the rest of the boys in fourth grade were gathered around me at recess as if I'd discovered an endless free source of baseball cards. For years I believed the story was true and could barely pass Alicia Franklin on the street without bursting out laughing. But then I heard it from two or three other, unconnected sources and figured out that, as brilliant as were most high-school male minds, it was unlikely that more than one would come up with that particular ploy and decided it must be an urban legend.

Under the guise of "local color" the main antagonist in *Running Loose*, Boomer Cowans, tells that same story. Louie Banks, the narrator of the tale, calls game on it the moment he hears it, and it serves to show that Boomer isn't exactly headed to England for his higher education. Many censors did not agree with the necessity of teaching that somewhat edgy lesson through the wonders of literature, and it led to my placement on a list in *USA Today* several summers ago as a top-ten banned author. It was the first and only time my name was being mentioned in the same sentence with Kurt Vonnegut and Mark Twain: heady stuff.

But it put me in the position of having to decide whether to keep the censors in my head as I grew and defined myself as a writer. I was already struggling with an idea some adults had about young adult literature: that its purpose should be to set examples rather than to reflect the truth as the author sees it. I was pretty sure I knew where I stood, given my perpetual state of arrested adolescence, but a four-year-old, mixed-race, neglected and abused girl gave me my answer in spades.

In my early years as a child and family therapist at the Spokane Mental Health Center, a job I began shortly after writing my first novel, I worked in an abuse and neglect project that included families with children under the age of five who had been treated so badly they'd been removed to foster care. Those families had to be minimally successful in our project in order to get the children back home.

Allie's mother had had a one-time sexual encounter with a black serviceman from the air force base, then engaged in a more permanent relationship with a racist short-haul truck driver. The first time I saw Allie, she was standing over the sink trying to wash the brown off her arms so she could be allowed to sit at the dinner table with her all-white half-brothers or play with toys they hadn't yet discarded.

Allie's life had been a nightmare by my standards, yet she presented as one of the most attractive children in the project. She was all muscle and sinew, could scale the walls like Spider-Man, but with a smile so wide and infectious that when she stood before you, arms outstretched, you *had* to pick her up. On that first day I did exactly that, and when

I raised her to eye level, she smiled even wider, looked right at me, and said, "Fuckerbitch." I was astonished enough to have no response other than to laugh. She said it again. I laughed again, and she laughed with me, and off we went to play.

At a break I caught the play therapist for a moment and said, "What's with 'fuckerbitch'?" She laughed, too. Funny stuff. "She uses it to see if you're safe," she said, and before she could explain that, some kid whacked another kid across the shoulder blades and she was off doing her job. For the second part of each day, I ran a group therapy session for the parents, and when Allie's parents began working on their issues, it was clear that their biggest was the existence of Allie, who was proof of the fact that her mother had had sexual relations with a black man, an unforgivable sin in the eyes of her stepfather. When things heated to the blowup point, you can guess which two words tumbled out of their mouths. Allie had merely combined them for convenience.

"When Allie hears those words," the play therapist said to me at our debriefing, "she knows the fight will end on her. She is living proof that her mother committed an unpardonable sin. So when she wants to discover whether or not an adult is safe, she simply runs those words up the flag-pole and gauges the response. Give her a negative reaction, she writes you out of her universe. If not, she gives you a chance."

Genius, if you think about it from the four-year-old perspective. Allie was key in shaping me as a writer. If I took those words away from her, she would have no way to test the waters, and though it's a pretty astonishing thing to hear roll off the tongue of a four-year-old, it would be nothing short of disrespectful to take away the language she needed to express her world. If I am to make characters real, I have to treat them with that same respect, and I have to be willing to tell stories about the ruggedness of their lives. Anything less is far more disrespectful than the use of those really meaningless words in print; disrespectful to the character, to the reader, and to the author. So anytime I get a character just right, find that spot where language and circumstance and character merge to tell some tough truth, I thank Allie. And because of her, I never back off the truth as I see it, or the language required to tell it.

From Chip Hilton
to Michael Jordan
and Beyond

14

A CHARACTER IN ONE OF MY BOOKS SAYS, "There is no act of heroism that doesn't include standing up for yourself." As a writer I'm always on the lookout for heroes. As a child and family therapist, that is also true. As a writer I need them to people my stories, to stand up against the bad guys, to grow from the first page of the first chapter to the last page of the last and know more about themselves at the end than they did at the beginning. I need them to supply hope in situations where others of us might shrink away. As a therapist I need them to do exactly the same things: to stand up in the face of shame, to find some piece within themselves that will help preserve them and their families from being torn apart by a system that can't accommodate them and a history that gives them little room to breathe.

Back before I entered junior high school, when it became so clear to me that books poison the mind (why else would they be offered up by the enemy?), I was enthralled, enraptured, mesmerized by Chip Hilton, creation of legendary basketball guru and sports fiction author Clair Bee. Chip was a made-to-order hero for me. I lived, as I've said, in a tiny lumber town of under a thousand people, situated in a high mountain valley in central Idaho, so isolated that the town's social schedule was set by the high-school football and basketball schedules. To a great degree the station of adults in the community fluctuated with the athletic ability of their male offspring. (I know my parents' status took a nasty dive with John's graduation.)

Chip Hilton was *good*. The unchallenged star of his football, basketball, and baseball teams throughout high school and college, he topped the academic honor role, worked late hours and weekends at the Sugar Bowl to help support his widowed mother, and was so morally upright that the bad guys at the outset of each book turned good by the last chapter and often led off as reformed bad guys in the first chapters of the next. I wanted to *be* Chip Hilton. He was tall, blond, and muscular, moved through his world on cat's paws. I was medium height with a cottage-cheese torso and a bad haircut my mother made me renew every two weeks just as it had grown out enough to darken my sidewalls sufficiently to rescue me from total dorkdom.

In sixth grade I discovered that with parental consent you could legally change your name. Since mine was a name my friends continually reminded me rhymed with a bathroom function, why wouldn't my parents allow me to change it to Chip Hilton? My dad said it might seem unusual, our last name being Crutcher and all. John (who I constantly reminded was named after a bathroom *fixture*) encouraged them to go ahead but to require that I change my middle name to Beef. The name change, of course, was not to be, but Chip Hilton remained my prepubescent hero, his friends Soapy Smith, Biggie Cohen, and Speed Morris, the gang I wanted to hang with.

But some funny things happened on my wildly circuitous route to and through adulthood. Through watching Cassius Clay renounce his "slave name" only to be stripped of his heavyweight boxing title and threatened with jail for refusing to go to war against a people who had "never called me nigger"; to seeing Tommy Smith and John Carlos atop the 1968 Olympic podium, heads bowed, black gloved fists raised in rigid salute; to watching a young burn victim at the city pool where I lifeguarded stand, horribly scarred, in his swimming suit, face and torso unrecognizable through the scars, patiently enduring the questions and taunts of his peers; to seeing a beautiful four-year-old stand before the sink day after day in play therapy, trying to wash the black off so her racist stepfather would allow her to touch the food and play with the toys and sit at the table with her all-white siblings, I realized that Chip Hilton wasn't brave.

Chip Hilton never had to prove he had a life worth living. Though his father was dead, his only memories were of the tall, smart, handsome man's love, his only job to carry on their good name.

Chip Hilton's life didn't include a father stopping by the tavern on his way home from a dead-end job, guzzling a six-pack, then taking his wife and kid to task when he arrived at home because the house wasn't cleaned to his specifications or dinner wasn't on the table.

Chip Hilton was never assaulted with gentle treachery in the after-midnight dark of his room, worried that the shadows in his imagination weren't in his imagination at all.

Chip Hilton didn't have to agonize over whether the girl of his dreams wouldn't go out with him because her parents couldn't accommodate the color of his skin or the shape of his facial features, or just because the girl had inherited that bigotry and made it her own.

Chip Hilton was like Superboy, and Superboy doesn't have to be brave because he's bulletproof. By the time I'd seen enough life to be able to write stories, I knew too many real heroes to allow myself to put Chip Hilton into them.

Don't get me wrong. There is certainly a place in literature for Chip and the Hardy Boys and Nancy Drew and Tom Swift. They tickle the imagination with possibilities: what could be, if only. They empower and excite. But as much as he represents something to aspire to, Chip also represents what can never be. A truth about humans is that we are a trial-and-error species; we learn from our mistakes, not just our physical mistakes but our emotional and spiritual mistakes as well. I think heroes aren't defined so much by what they do "right," as by how they respond to what they do "wrong."

If I have any complaints about my youth, and if you've read this far you know I have many, one is that so many well-meaning adults lied to me. Not spiteful lies with malicious intent but lies designed to prevent emotional and psychological pain, lies told by the people who cared about me most: my parents, teachers, relatives. They were lies designed to prevent disappointment, lies about the virtues of love, hard work, and any number of terms around which clichés blossom like desert flowers after a flash flood. They were meant to pave my way to Chip Hiltonhood. And I believed them, and became disillusioned when life turned out to operate by a different set of rules. Love brought as many problems as it solved. It didn't "conquer all"; it challenged, it tested. Honesty was the best policy, unless you didn't want someone to know the truth.

In 1964 I was a freshman in college, swimming distance for the Eastern Washington State College swim team (and wondering how I could ever exist in academia without my brother's homework, which had propelled me through high school). The varsity locker room at Eastern was a sprawling, semiopen space accommodating all the in-season athletes. I sat before my locker one day, psyching myself up for the grueling workout ahead, listening to the basketball players at the lockers behind me spinning their prepractice yarns.

There was in the state of Washington at the time a small-high-school basketball coach legendary for his number of postseason victories. One of the players on Eastern's freshman squad had played for this coach and was telling how he believed they had won the state championship the previous year. According to the player, their "team of destiny" was about to be knocked off track early in the season because a "ringer" had been brought onto a competing team in their league. The player was black. The coach pulled the doors closed on a team meeting and told his players that he had played with *them* in college and the only way to stop *them* was to hurt *them*. He wanted the kid out of the game by halftime.

To make a long story short, he got his wish and the team fulfilled its destiny and the coach continued free on his march to athletic sainthood. I truly expected at least one of the Eastern players on the other side of those lockers to kick the storyteller's butt or at least voice an opinion on what a monumental jerk he was. I heard only laughter—laughter and agreement. I'm ashamed to this day that I didn't go around there and voice an opinion myself. But I was afraid to get hurt and even more afraid to get embarrassed.

Seventeen years later when I sat down to write my first novel, fueled by heroes of literature such as Atticus Finch and Boo Radley and Holden Caulfield and Billy Pilgrim, I created Louie Banks, the flawed hero of *Running Loose*, who took at least three runs at integrity before finally willing himself to do what I lacked the courage for back in that locker room in 1964. There was no Chip Hilton in that story, but Louie Banks was able to find the edges of some truths that had eluded Chris Crutcher.

Since then I have searched for my heroes among the

small-t truths. I always find them among people learning the art of acceptance: not acceptance of defeat or acceptance of some inability to influence their own futures, but rather acceptance of life on the planet, acceptance of the grays rather than the black-and-whites, acceptance of the astonishing range of human emotion and human behavior.

Before his death from AIDS, tennis great Arthur Ashe did an ESPN interview with Roy Firestone. After plumbing the depths of the certain and awful realities ahead, Roy asked Arthur if he ever asked, "Why me?" Arthur looked directly into his eyes, and in that soft, powerful tone that became the very meaning of dignity before his death, he said, "Why not me?" Arthur Ashe told us a simple truth about the world. Viruses have no morality, no sense of good and evil, the deserving or the undeserving. Open an avenue for them and they go down it. AIDS is not the swift sword with which the Lord punishes the evil practitioners of male homosexuality and intravenous drug use. It is simply an opportunistic virus that does what it has to do to stay alive. Living, I believe Arthur was telling us, is risky. If one of my protagonists discovers the truth as Arthur Ashe tells it, he or she attains the status of hero.

A common point of argument these days is whether or not we should hold sports figures up as role models or heroes. Charles Barkley stated on repeated occasions during his playing days that "role model" was not his job; he was a basketball player. Barkley has always been one to openly admit his failings, which in my mind makes him a good role model; he tells the truth about who he believes he is.

An even tighter focus in that regard was—and still is—put on Michael Jordan. Is Michael a role model? A hero of our time? Let me tell you why I believe he is. Michael's heroism, in my mind, has little to do with his ability to find that air step three-quarters of the way to the hoop that allows him to stay in the air a split second longer than all other members of his species, or his ability to score more than forty points when his body is racked with flu, or even his ability to take a year off from the NBA and return better than when he left. Those are simply attributes of Superman.

Here's one thing that makes Michael a hero to me: During the O. J. Simpson trial, Fred Goldman, father of slain Ron Goldman, showed up in court every day, expressed his rage to the press on a regular basis, and declared he would be there every day in search of justice for his slain son. When justice was not found, in his view, he was more outraged than ever and he let us know it. His idea of righteousness was to not rest until his son's death was avenged.

I don't want to take away from Fred Goldman's grief.

His loss was devastating. But on a scale of one to ten for violent deaths and undeserved loss in this country, Ron Goldman's death rates maybe a six.

Michael's father, arguably every bit as loved by Michael as Ron was by Fred, also died a violent, senseless death. A couple of two-bit hoodlums came upon him sleeping in his car and killed him for whatever money and valuables were on his person. Michael Jordan didn't spend one day in that courtroom. He didn't call for the death penalty or demand that the justice system exact retribution for him. When asked about his feelings for his father's killers or what should happen to them, in the only recount I ever heard, all he said was, "My father is dead. That's all I care about." There it is again. *My place as a god in the sports world doesn't give me favored status in the eyes of the universe.*

Every human who loves runs the risk of loss; the greater the love, the greater the loss. When the Bulls won the championship in the year following his father's death, Michael collapsed in tears, overcome by the perfect juxtaposition of unimagined glory and crushing heartache. In that moment the extremes of existence brought him to the floor, and he was humbled. He showed us who he was, and we saw it and we were humbled with him. Any protagonist I create to "Be like Mike" will be like Mike in that way.

I was sitting in my small mental health center office one day in the late eighties, catching up on some client charts, when a man in his early twenties appeared in my doorway. He asked if I was Chris Crutcher. I had helped a friend of his, he said, who had been involved with Child Protective Services. In those days the center was a take-the-first-available-therapist kind of place with very little capability for matching therapists with appropriate clients. I asked if he had checked in at the front desk, and he said he had just walked through the halls till he saw my name.

"Actually, they don't allow you to do that," I said. "You have to put your name on an intake list."

He said, "I'm here, aren't I?"

Hard to argue. "Don't worry," he said. "I can pay you."

It was interesting he showed up when he did; I seldom had a free hour. He closed the door and proceeded to tell me that he had "vegetableized" his child. His family was so famous in our town, he told me, that if a cop saw him or one of his brothers driving down the street at the speed limit, buckled up, they still had probable cause to pull them over. He had fallen in love with his wife when they were both still in school, and they had married. His only real job had been dealing drugs, and she had made him promise to stop if she married him. They had a little girl, but Jonah couldn't get a real job because his rap sheet was long as a fat man's grocery list, so Deeana took two fast-food jobs to bring in enough money to live, and Jonah was charged with caring for their daughter.

"She cried all the time," he said. "My wife walked out the door and she started crying and I couldn't shut her up for more than fifteen minutes at a time till Deeana got back. I felt like a shit, you know. I should have been out there making a living while Deeana took care of the kid. I swear to god the minute Deeana would walk back in that door, Shauna would shut up. I started thinking the kid hated me.

"I already knew I had trouble with my temper," he went on, "but I was doing pretty good. When things got too bad, I'd lock myself in the bathroom until I could pull it together, then go back out there and perform my matronly duties."

I knew what was coming. Using willpower to control rage is like building a house with a ball-peen hammer and thumbtacks.

"One night Deeana comes home and I'm out back smoking a little dope to calm myself down 'cause Shauna has been bawling and fussing even more than usual, and Deeana gets on my case because I'm not watching her. I am, just from a distance. We get into a fight and then Deeana tells me she picked up another shift. We need the money, but I don't want her to go because I'm about to the end of me. Shauna shut up the second Deeana walked in, as always, and she started up again the second Deeana walked out."

He stopped and gripped the arms of the chair. "I gave her the bottle and checked her drawers and nothing was wrong, but she just wouldn't shut the hell up. I should have walked off; I didn't want to hit her, you know, but I was a little too far gone, so I just kind of grabbed her and . . . " His voice trailed off.

"You shook her," I said.

"Yeah."

"Where is she now?"

"This place in New Mexico," he said.

"Did you go to jail?"

"Sure did."

"How long?" I asked.

"Not as long as I should have. Six months. I'm still on parole."

I took a deep breath. "So, what do you want to do?"

He took a deeper breath. "It's what I don't want to do," he said. "Deeana's pregnant again."

Oh, *man*. "You guys are still together?" Not many relationships withstand this incident. Not many *should*.

"Yeah," he said. "We're still together. Been apart a

couple times . . . " He looked at the stack of charts on my desk. "You can't be writing any of this down," he said.

"I don't have a choice," I said. "I'm already famous around here for not having my charts up to date."

"Then this should make you immortal. Actually, I don't want anyone even knowing I'm here. I'll pay you straight out cash."

I said the center didn't allow us to do private practice from there.

"You can do anything you want in this place," he said. "Nobody knows."

I asked how it was he knew so much about this place.

"You kidding? No matter what else I got sentenced to, growing up, I always got sentenced to here. Law figures they got to put you in counseling if you pee in a doorway." He didn't hold counseling in particularly high esteem. I said that.

"Hey, man," he said. "You ever checked this place out . . . I mean, get to know your colleagues? Hell, I bet I've stormed out of more doors in this place than you know exist."

He was right. It was a real crapshoot when a client came through intake. The center was where people went who had the means for nothing else.

"But you're here."

"That's because my buddy told me about you. He said it helped."

I reminded him that that particular buddy ended up leaving his family so the kids wouldn't be removed.

"I know that," he said. "But he said coming here helped him see he didn't have a chance, that it was best for his old lady and kids if he just stepped away."

He was right. His friend had at least left with less rage and a better understanding of his anger; a knowledge that he probably wasn't going to get it under control and would, without divine intervention, be dangerous to his family if the stars lined up right. Like everything else, success is relative.

"Okay," I said. "You don't want to be leaving tracks all over the mental health center. I'm assuming Child Protective Services knows your wife is having another baby. Are there stipulations; are they requiring you to move out when the baby comes?"

He shook his head. "I completed the anger management classes they made me take and went through a program through the department of corrections. I'm cured." He said the word with a certain amount of sarcasm.

"So what do you want?"

He said, "I want to make sure I don't hurt this new baby."

Within a very few sessions it was clear Jonah was less risk to his new baby than he feared, and a lot less risk than many guys who would be allowed around their kids. His sense of regret and shame was so great that it was highly unlikely he would let himself get that far out of control again; plus, he had thought at the time that shaking the child was a lot less dangerous than hitting her, which is, of course, not true, but which said he could call on a certain amount of restraint. He also had learned to keep himself out of situations that could lead to long periods of caring for the new baby alone. He had gone back to selling drugs on a limited basis, and Deeana would be the primary caretaker for the new baby.

Our job was to help him find a way to live with himself. While his rage was—while nearly all rage is—focused on self, his was now *clearly* focused on himself. The amount and intensity of self-contempt for what he had done was palpable, and at its greatest intensity he was in danger of losing almost any relationship he might have. We worked through his life: Received his allowance in grass—marijuana—from the time he was six years old, could sell it or smoke it. Held the record for being the youngest child ever locked up in juvy—eight. Thrown out of school at least three times per year up until his freshman year in high school, when he took the hint and simply didn't go back (though he was more knowledgable and articulate than many high-school or even college graduates I've known). Everything about him smacked of loss, of *not good enough*. Left by his father, neglected by his mother, ass kicked by his brothers. He spoke of Deeana as if she were a fairy-tale goddess, far prettier than he deserved, far smarter than he deserved, far more honest, and far more loyal. She gave him a family, and he broke it.

"She's just down there," he said of his firstborn. "She'll never be any better or any different; just bigger. Deeana and I stayed down there awhile. After I got out of jail, I went to see her every day, but finally Deeana made me stop because most times I couldn't quit crying, and when I did, I'd get mean, like I was trying to make her leave me as some kind of punishment. I hated my own wife because she was willing to be with me after what I did."

The baby was born. Jonah was very uneasy. He loved her with the same fury as the guilt that ravaged him. Weekly we met, and weekly we stayed in exactly the same place. I don't know how many times I required a nonsuicide pact before letting him walk out of the room. Deeana came in with him several times, carrying her beautiful, soft, gurgling baby, and Jonah would sit in the far corner of the office and stare.

Finally one week when he came in alone, I said, "Jonah, we have to figure what we can salvage here."

"Well, I'm not forgiving myself, you can forget that."

"That's up to you, but we still have to salvage something. You've got another little girl there. You've got a wife. They're waiting for you, Jonah."

"Maybe I ought to leave."

"And maybe you will," I said. "But you came here for a reason. We haven't talked about one thing you didn't already know before you came in. And you came anyway."

"I think I have to leave."

I said, "And go where?"

"Streets," he said. "Back to dealing full-time, I guess. I can make a lot of money doing that, keep Deeana and Shyla in style."

"Some style," I said. "Living on drug money that could dry up in a second because the old man gets busted. Tell you what, before you decide on that path, you think long and hard. I want you to come back when you've thought of one thing we can salvage. If you haven't come up with it by this time next week, don't come in; wait until you do. If you come up with it this afternoon, call and I'll get you in. Whenever. The next thing you and I are going to talk about is what you can salvage."

Two days later he called, and I canceled my next client.

"I know what it is, Doc." He knew I wasn't a Ph.D.

"Shoot."

"It's not much. . . ."

"Shoot. It's more than we had two days ago."

"It's this. Now it isn't worth it, and you'd never prescribe it, but . . . Shyla's going to have a lot better dad because of what I did. There's nothing I can do about Shauna now. Nothing. But I can give Shyla everything I was going to give her anyway, and everything I was going to give Shauna. I mean everything. All the love. All the toys. All the clothes."

He was quiet a minute, waiting for me.

"One more thing. I can give her mother the same. I can work and hold my temper and love her and make sure she gets to go to chiropractic school and whatever else because that will make her a better mother because she'll be happy." He waited again. Then, "Well, what do you think?"

I said it was more than I could have thought of, which was the truth. I said it was the best.

"It won't stop hurting," he said.

I agreed.

Jonah stood up and shook my hand, and that was the last time I saw him. I wish I thought his predictions all came true, that he provided and loved and gave his way to redemption. If that's true, however, it would be my first experience with that. More likely he limped along doing his best when he could find the best in himself. Statistically, his chances of making it with his family aren't good. But he lives in my writing heart. A hero is only a hero for the moment, only a hero when he can sift through the pieces of his life and find something to hold on to, something that is him.

So my heroes are like Jonah and they're like Michael Jordan on his knees *after* the heroics, showing us who he is. They're Chris Crutcher with the balls to pull on that coonskin cap one more time, believing he can turn his pimply face into that of a rugged frontiersman. They're Jewell Crutcher living her final seventeen years in sobriety, brought on by the fear of never being able to care for her grandchildren. They're Arthur Ashe having lost his physical grace to the ravages of a coldhearted virus, only to show twice that grace in his humanness. They're twenty years of men and women forced by the law or child protective services to come to the mental health center for "help" who finally stood up and said what they did and who they were. What an amazing place I've been given to stand and watch. What a rich pool for stories.

Epilogue

————◆◆◆————

WHEN MY NEW EDITOR, Virginia Duncan, finished reading the foregoing chapters, she quickly e-mailed me with: "You write about athletes and athletics all the time. You still play basketball; you've even entered triathlons. How did you get from the dweeb I read about to what you are today? Something is missing." I wrote back: "Hey, nobody told me an autobiography had to contain the truth. Jeez."

I do sign off on those foregoing chapters as true to the best of my knowlege under penalty of perjury, but of course there's more. Living in Cascade, Idaho, was like living in a Larry McMurtry novel, only it was small-town North instead of small-town South. There were precious few avenues to "become." I grew up idolizing athletes from Mickey Mantle to Michael Jordan, but none of those superstars stands any taller or takes up any more space in my memory than Jack Hull and Dick Earl and Jerry Ready and Dave Lowry and the Bilbaos and the Hirais: the guys who stood on the Rambler sideline, helmets in hand, sweat running from their foreheads, nodding at the coach, then tearing back to the huddle with the plan that would bring our purple-and-gold eight-man football team to triumph. These guys brought hundreds of our townsfolk out on the dark, freezing nights of the long Idaho winter to watch them go to hoop wars with the Vandals or the Rangers or the Lumberjacks. Some of my best grade-school memories are of simply standing around after a game, listening to those guys recount their heroics. But it was hard to measure up. With a July birthday I was young for my grade, *and* what little athletic DNA flowed over the generations splashed mostly on my brother, John, and my sister, Candy.

My ninth year, 1955, was the first year of organized Little League in Cascade. I already knew from playing backyard baseball with the kids in my neighborhood that I wasn't much of a ballplayer. I couldn't keep my eye on the ball at bat or in the field. When I saw it coming in my direction, it might as well have been a bullet. But everyone was excited when the adults began forming teams, and I had to be excited, too. I wasn't hot for practices or games, but I couldn't wait to get a pair of cleats to hang over one handlebar and a glove to hang over the other, and though we weren't allowed to wear our T-shirts anywhere but to games, we could wear the caps anywhere, and the idea of being identified as a member of a sports team was about as good an idea as there was.

I started working for my dad at the service station that summer, and though my parents always worked hard to make ends meet, the paycheck I earned might have made me the richest kid my age in town. My folks required me to deposit half my paycheck in the bank for future college tuition—or bail money, whichever came first—but the other half was mine to spend as I pleased. I talked myself into believing I would be a much better ballplayer if I had primo equipment, and down at the Cascade Merc, which is like a general store, was a genuine leather, Warren Spahn-autograph model baseball glove. I would have much preferred a Mickey Mantle or Willie Mays model, but Warren Spahn was what they had and Warren Spahn was what I saved for. I waited through three paychecks, bought far less candy and no forty-five rock-and-roll records. I dreamed about that glove, saw the tiny horsehide growing as it came toward me from the sky, then landed with a plop in the webbing, saw my teammates cheering and slapping my back. When I'd finally saved the dough, I pedaled down to the Merc, walked through the front door, and laid hard cold cash on the counter in front of Bob Gardner, later of Fourth of July fame. My brother showed me how to massage the glove with neat's-foot oil to soften and toughen the leather, then gave me a hardball to place in the webbing so I could wrap the glove in twine overnight to form the perfect pocket. For the first three games of the season I'd used one of John's old gloves out in right field, and though I hadn't come within ten yards of catching a fly ball, this was going to change things. Warren Spahn, whoever he was, wouldn't let me down.

I hung the glove on my handlebars and pedaled all over town the day of the next game, hoping people would notice. None did, but undaunted I showed up early at the field to play catch with anyone who would throw the ball with me, then took outfield practice when the other players began to arrive.

Just after Coach turned in his batting order, he called me in, put his hand on my shoulder, and said, "Chris, Charles forgot his glove tonight and we don't have anyone here to go get it. It's a lot more important to have a glove on second base than in right field, so I want you to give him yours just for this game." I stood speechless. I don't think Coach knew the glove was new or had any idea what was happening inside me. "Stand farther back than usual," he said. "You can always run up on a ball faster than you can go back to get it. Don't worry about catching the fly balls; you haven't been too successful at that anyway. Just don't let anything get behind you."

Charles Boots stood waiting for my glove. I handed it over and turned to hustle to right field so no one would see the tears streaming down my face. I stood way, way back, almost to the jungle gym; Julio Bilbao or Gary Hirai couldn't have put one behind me. I stood there, hating Charles for being so stupid as to forget his glove, imagining he knew mine was new and that Coach would let him use it if he left his dried, cracked, no-pocket, no-autograph piece-of-shit glove on his back porch. I vowed to become a famous athlete and come back to this town and sign not one autograph, except for the next poor schmuck they stuck in right field because he couldn't catch a cold, much less a fly ball. I hated everyone: Charles for being stupid, Coach for taking the glove, my parents for letting me buy it in the first place. But mostly I hated myself. I hated myself for not being good enough to play where I'd need a glove. I *ached* to be good.

Fact is, in baseball it was not to be. I never had the reflexes for it and could never redefine a hardball as anything other than a hard leather projectile launched to hurt me. By the time Ellen Breidenbach batted out my teeth at fourteen, I'd had enough. But I didn't shine all that much at the other sports, either. Determination and temper turned me into a pretty good hitter on the football field by the time I was a senior, but I never had the speed or agility for high-school basketball, and only shone at track when the fast guys graduated.

I never lost that ache. In college I joined the fledgling swim team and turned my body over to the G. Gordon Liddy, the Bobby Knight of swim coaches, and used the memory of my athletic embarrassments to push me until I gained respectability on desire alone. During the two years I taught in a public high school, I befriended the basketball coach, a fabulous athlete named Randy Dolven, who had played basketball in Europe after college, and let him coach me as he might one of his high-school players, picking up skills I would have died for back in my teens. I took those skills to the outdoor court, playing three-on-three basketball at least five days a week on the concrete courts of Berkeley. My grandmother's and mother's obsession with counting each and every calorie that passed your lips, coupled with the demand to clean every crumb from your plate, kept me running and/or swimming daily from the time I graduated college until this very day. It was the only way to burn off the calories. If you burned more, you could eat more. Somewhere in time, accelerated heartbeats and sweat-soaked T-shirts simply became habit. I'm nearly fifty-six as I write this and am probably still three times the athlete I was in high school.

But sometimes on the court, or three miles out on a run, or ten hundred-yard freestyle sprints into a set of fifteen, I allow myself to become young again, to let my imagination create an arena where *I'm* Jack Hull or Julio Bilbao or Gary Hirai, where some young kid is standing in awe of me as I pull on my helmet and sprint back to the huddle, where I call the play. I can never tell that hero's story, however, without also telling the story of the young, ungifted ballplayer, his imagination full of wishes, pedaling down the dusty backstreets of Cascade, not knowing necessarily that they'll take his glove, but that they might.

For every bit of humor and compassion I put into a story, I put in an equal dose of anger. The athletic backdrops to my stories are significant to me because of the struggle athletics has always provided. I look back and wish my athletic mentors had been able to present a larger picture and had celebrated the sport relative to the ability of the individual athlete. I wish they had made it clean, wish they hadn't made it patriotic, religious, moral. A sport has its own built-in integrity, doesn't need an artificial one. Athletics carries its own set of truths, and those truths are diminished when manipulated by people with agendas. So, in my stories, I let my characters try to find the purity, the juxtaposition of mind, body, and spirit that I discovered in athletics at a much later age.

There is as much missing from this autobiography as there is written, but I suppose that's the way it has to be. Random chance as much as anything else dictated what I was thinking each day when I brought myself to the keyboard, and who knows what forces dictated its direction from there. What I know from writing it is this: As predictable as life seems, as many times as I have done things over and over and over, hoping for a different result, it is, in fact, not predictable. In my youth I could never have imagined seeing my name on a book unless I had carved it there with a sharp instrument, could never have predicted the nature of the humans who would turn out to be my friends or my enemies, those who would teach me or those who would hold me down. And I could never, *never* have imagined that in the last half of the decade of my fifties, I would own a genuine coonskin cap.　　◆

An Ill-Advised Photo Album

I'd be a better cowboy if they let me get rid of the bib overalls

Alone with "The Lone Ranger"

Getting ready to "do something neat"

Future triathlete on his balloon-tired Schwinn one-speed

123-pound offensive guard, striking fear into all who would oppose me

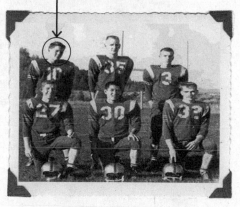

Senior players on the 1963–64 Cascade Ramblers eight-man high school football team

So the football thing didn't work out—how about swimming?

1966–67 Eastern Washington State College savage swim team

259

Headed for the 1960 National Boy Scout jamboree, posing as a real *Boy Scout*

1964 high school graduate and future business tycoon—it didn't quite work out

King of the Mild Frontier

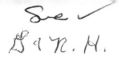

A LAND
REMEMBERED

*Novels by
    Patrick D. Smith*

The River Is Home
The Beginning
Forever Island
Angel City
Allapattah
A Land Remembered